HEIDEGGER'S WAY O

In *Heidegger's Way of Being*, the follow-up to his 2010 book, *Engaging Heidegger*, Richard Capobianco clearly and compellingly makes the case that the core matter of Heidegger's lifetime of thought was Being as the temporal emergence of all beings and things. Drawing upon a wide variety of texts, many of which have been previously untranslated, Capobianco illuminates the overarching importance of Being as radiant manifestation – "the truth of Being" – and how Heidegger also named and elucidated this fundamental phenomenon as Nature-*physis*, *Aletheia*, the primordial *Logos*, and as *Ereignis*, *Lichtung*, and *Es gibt*.

Heidegger's Way of Being brings back into full view the originality and distinctiveness of Heidegger's thought and offers an emphatic rejoinder to certain more recent readings, and particularly those that propose a reduction of Being to "sense" or "meaning" and maintain that the core matter is human meaning-making. Capobianco's vivid and often poetic reflections serve to evoke for readers the very experience of Being – or as he prefers to name it, the Being-way – and to invite us to pause and meditate on the manner of our human way in relation to the Being-way.

(New Studies in Phenomenology and Hermeneutics)

RICHARD CAPOBIANCO is a professor in the Department of Philosophy at Stonehill College.

New Studies in Phenomenology and Hermeneutics

Kenneth Maly, General Editor

New Studies in Phenomenology and Hermeneutics aims to open up new approaches to classical issues in phenomenology and hermeneutics. Thus its intentions are the following: to further the work of Edmund Husserl, Maurice Merleau-Ponty, and Martin Heidegger, as well as that of Paul Ricoeur, Hans-Georg Gadamer, and Emmanuel Levinas; to enhance phenomenological thinking today by means of insightful interpretations of texts in phenomenology as they inform current issues in philosophical study; to inquire into the role of interpretation in phenomenological thinking; to take seriously Husserl's term *phenomenology* as "a science which is intended to supply the basic instrument for a rigorously scientific philosophy and, in its consequent application, to make possible a methodical reform of all the sciences"; to take up Heidegger's claim that "what is own to phenomenology, as a philosophical 'direction,' does not rest in being *real*. Higher than reality stands *possibility*. Understanding phenomenology consists solely in grasping it as possibility"; and to practise *phenomenology* as "underway," as "the *praxis* of the self-showing of the matter for thinking," as "entering into the movement of enactment-thinking."

The commitment of this book series is also to provide English translations of significant works from other languages. In summary, **New Studies in Phenomenology and Hermeneutics** intends to provide a forum for a full and fresh thinking and rethinking of the way of phenomenology and interpretive phenomenology, that is, hermeneutics.

For a list of books published in the series, see page 123.

Heidegger's Way of Being

RICHARD CAPOBIANCO

UNIVERSITY OF TORONTO PRESS
Toronto Buffalo London

© University of Toronto Press 2014
Toronto Buffalo London
www.utppublishing.com
Printed in the U.S.A.

Reprinted in paperback 2015

ISBN 978-1-4426-4963-7 (cloth)
ISBN 978-1-4426-3069-7 (paper)

Printed on acid-free, 100% post-consumer recycled paper.

Library and Archives Canada Cataloguing in Publication

Capobianco, Richard, 1957–, author
Heidegger's way of being / Richard Capobianco.

(New studies in phenomenology and hermeneutics)
Includes bibliographical references and indexes.
ISBN 978-1-4426-4963-7 (bound). – ISBN 978-1-4426-3069-7 (paperback)

1. Heidegger, Martin, 1889–1976. 2. Ontology. 3. Philosophy,
Modern – 20th century. I. Title. II. Title: Way of being. III. Series:
New studies in phenomenology and hermeneutics (Toronto, Ont.)

B3279.H49C369 2014   193   C2014-904291-4

University of Toronto Press acknowledges the financial assistance to
its publishing program of the Canada Council for the Arts and the
Ontario Arts Council, an agency of the Government of Ontario.

 Canada Council   Conseil des Arts
for the Arts   du Canada

ONTARIO ARTS COUNCIL
CONSEIL DES ARTS DE L'ONTARIO
an Ontario government agency
un organisme du gouvernement de l'Ontario

University of Toronto Press acknowledges the financial support of
the Government of Canada through the Canada Book Fund for its
publishing activities.

To emerge and be of the sky, of the sun and moon and flying clouds, as one with them.

Walt Whitman, from "A Song of Joys"

Contents

Acknowledgments

To my cherished family.

To Marie Göbel for her delight in the music of language; Dieter Schönecker for his boundless enthusiasm for philosophical thinking; and Gábor Ferge, editor of the journal *Existentia* (Budapest), for his passion for the beautiful word and image and for originally publishing articles that now appear, updated and expanded, as chapters 2, 3, 5, and 6: *Existentia* 22 (2012): 15–23 and 177–86; *Existentia* 23 (2013): 65–76 and 201–12.

To colleagues, near and far, and my students, now and then; to Len Husband, Wayne Herrington, and the terrific team at the University of Toronto Press; to Betsy Dean; and to Stonehill College for the financial support for this project.

~⁓⁓⁓~

And to the singer of the songs I have always heard most vividly, perhaps because I, too, started from Paumanok.

HEIDEGGER'S WAY OF BEING

Introduction

Above all I wish that ... undisguised nature addresses
you and that through it you are claimed by what
never ceases to claim human beings.
                    Heidegger in a letter to Paul Hassler, 1967[1]

The studies in this volume, which continue and develop the
basic themes that I sounded in my earlier book *Engaging Heidegger*, focus on that which never ceases to address us human
beings – Being – the fundamental matter of Heidegger's lifetime
of thinking.[2]

In a contemporary world that leaves less and less room for
the kind of "meditative thinking" that Heidegger called for,
these studies celebrate his efforts and celebrate the peculiar
beauty and wisdom of a contemplative comportment towards
all beings and things in their temporal-spatial unfolding. Such
released thinking clearly goes against the contemporary grain
of our busy, "connected" world; but as well, it also appears to
go against the grain of much of contemporary Heidegger study
and scholarship. In recent years there has been an increasing
interest in how Heidegger's thought can be related to all sorts
of practical social, political, environmental, and design concerns, and while these efforts have yielded interesting and even
helpful results, the matter of Being has been almost entirely
left behind. Or if not set aside in this way, then in the work of

other recent Heidegger commentators, the question of Being has been transformed into the question of "meaning," and the "meaning-making" activity of the human being has taken centre stage in the scholarship. In these accounts, *Sein* is reducible to *Sinn*, and Heidegger's thinking is brought so close to Husserl's that there remains hardly a trace of the profound and fundamental difference between the two approaches that Heidegger insisted upon. To be sure, Heidegger was intensively concerned with human Dasein's "languaged" relation to Being, and the studies that follow point this out again and again, but what I have made every effort to show, beginning in chapter 1, is that his paramount concern was with the *primacy of Being* in relation to human Dasein.[3]

Heidegger was indeed determined to "overcome" the atemporal understanding of "being" as "beingness" (*ousia*, substance, *essentia*, essence) that had dominated Western metaphysical thinking since Plato, but we must also keep in mind that his very turn to the matter of *Being* was more immediately prompted by the prevailing tendency in the modern tradition of the philosophy of consciousness to relate everything back to the *logos* of the human being. In other words, from Descartes to Husserl he detected the ascendency and triumph of the philosophical position that views "what is" principally in terms of the meaning-constituting or sense-making activity of the human *logos*. It was this decisive turn in modern philosophy to the human *logos* – and to the preoccupation with "meaning" – that he sought to counter by a decisive *return* to the question of *Being*.

For Heidegger, *Sein* had been largely "forgotten" in the turn to *Sinn*, and this made raising anew the *Seinsfrage* so important and even urgent. To overcome this preoccupation with the noetic in modern and contemporary philosophy (Husserl's "phenomenology" included), he was resolved to bring back into view, by way of a retrieval of ancient Greek experience, thinking, and poetizing, "the manifestation of Being" (*die Offenbarkeit des Seins*) or "the truth of Being" (*die Wahrheit des Seins*). Being as *physis* as *aletheia*. He called upon us to recall that only insofar as there is manifestation, emergence, is there meaning at all. Thus, Being *qua* manifestation is structurally prior to, and the ontological condition of, meaning. Being structurally precedes and exceeds meaning. Being is irreducible to meaning.

Heidegger therefore set for himself this formidable task in relation to the modern Cartesian tradition of thinking, and he accomplished it from beginning to end in his own distinctive, and some might say eccentric, way. He was guided by his own muse, to be sure, and his body of work is not philosophical in any usual sense of the word. For some, his turn, or return, to the matter of Being is both philosophically significant and existentially profound and far-reaching. For others, his basic philosophical point was blunted by the strangeness and obscurity of his rhetoric. There is truth in both takes, I might admit, but what we cannot mistake is the brilliance and originality of his philosophical voice and vision. For this reason alone we ought to make every effort to understand his manifold attempts, over the course of a long lifetime, to say and thereby show the proper character of Being – the *Ur*-phenomenon that in his view the ancient Greeks named *physis*, *aletheia*, the primordial *Logos*, *hen*, and that he creatively and poetically named *Ereignis*, *Lichtung*, *Gegend* (*Gegnet*), and *Es gibt*. These studies offer a sympathetic – but also a careful and rigorous – reading of Heidegger's ways and byways of thinking Being, and my aim is always to try to understand and appreciate what he is seeing in the saying.

The dates of the texts I address range widely, from 1919 to shortly before his death in 1976. Throughout, I have sought to examine passages that have been largely overlooked or underappreciated in the scholarship, and, in fact, all of the chapters include considerable material from volumes of the *Gesamtausgabe* (Heidegger's *Complete Works*) that have not yet been translated. These texts shed new light on his thinking and offer compelling new evidence that the Being-question was always the *Grund*-question for Heidegger. Chapter 2 introduces readers to a beautiful little meditation, composed by Heidegger after 1970, on several of Hölderlin's "last poems." Here we encounter the quintessential "later" Heidegger refiguring and restating important matters – such as *time* – that had long been central to his thinking. What is more, he takes up in a new way what he had considered in the early 1940s to be Hölderlin's special insight into

"Nature," and we discern in his elucidation of the "last poems" that Hölderlin's "Nature" is indeed but another name for Being itself (*Sein selbst*). This chapter thus sets into play the motif of Being as Nature-*physis* as *aletheia* that is also the concern of the following two chapters, and in chapter 4, I emphasize the critical importance of his discussion of *physis* in his 1935 *Introduction to Metaphysics* – the text that I maintain is his true masterwork of the 1930s. Chapters 5 and 6 focus on his two thematically rich lecture courses on Heraclitus in 1943 and 1944 respectively (both of which, surprisingly, have not yet been translated into English even though the volume was published in the German in 1979), and I bring attention to passages and themes that are not to be found in the better-known essays that were composed and published later in the 1950s.[4] These two lecture courses reveal to us several important and distinctive features of Heidegger's thinking, including how he worked out in a brilliant if enigmatic way the proper character of the "word" within the proper "relation" (*Bezug, Beziehung*) between the human being and Being (as *physis* and as the primordial *Logos*).

For Heidegger, what calls for and calls forth thinking is Being. It is my task to keep this fully in our view. My hope is that, taken together, the studies in this volume will offer readers a philosophical and poetic meditation on his way of Being that not only elucidates but also evokes the *experience* of Being – or, as I prefer to name it, the Being-way.

Chapter 1

Reaffirming "The Truth of Being"

Aletheia is ... the fundamental feature of Being itself.

Lecture course on Heraclitus, 1943

Truth abides in everything that abides.

Lecture course on Parmenides, 1942–3

Over the past several decades, Heidegger's thinking has been appropriated or expropriated, as it were, in myriad ways, and all of these various approaches testify to the extraordinary reach and richness of his thought. Yet the time has come to bring back into view the core matter of his thinking. William J. Richardson tells the story (and the late Manfred Frings related a similar story) of his visit with Heidegger in his home in Zähringen (Freiburg) in 1959. At one point in their discussion, Heidegger, gazing out the window of his study and contemplating the wooded landscape, expressed his desire, his eagerness, to say "it" yet again. What was the "it" that Heidegger – for a whole lifetime – had his eyes upon? This "it" (*es*) that "gives" (*gibt*) so richly and so inexhaustibly is Being itself (*Sein selbst*) as the temporal-spatial emerging and shining-forth of beings in their beingness as gathered in the ensemble. Being as "manifestness" or "manifestation" (*Offenbarkeit*), this is the matter itself (*die Sache selbst*) of Heidegger's thought – which, remarkably enough, is at risk of being "forgotten" all over again. A

Seinsvergessenheit is settling in anew – and in Heidegger studies of all places. Over the last decade there has been a trend in the Heidegger scholarship towards understanding Being as reducible to "meaning" ("sense"), that is, towards understanding Being only in terms of Dasein's constitutive meaning-making activity.[1] Yet *die Sache:* not principally Dasein, but *Sein qua manifestation – what Heidegger came to call "the truth of Being"* – in relation to Dasein.

I.   An Early Clue

In the 1960s, Heidegger repeatedly emphasized in his work and in his personal correspondence that it was the "manifestness" of Being that had guided his thinking from the start.[2] In 1973, three years before his death, in a seminar with French colleagues in Zähringen, he made the observation that whereas Husserl was influenced primarily by the Brentano of the 1874 work *Psychology from an Empirical Standpoint*, he himself, from the very beginning of his *Denkweg,* had been propelled by Brentano's 1862 study *On the Manifold Meaning of Being in Aristotle.* In the seminar, as the protocol has it, Heidegger added with a smile – but with emphasis: "My Brentano is the Brentano of Aristotle!"[3]

What Heidegger was pointing to was that in his view, Husserl, despite his breakthrough to the "things themselves" – and while there remains considerable debate about this matter, let us grant that there was a break out of the Cartesian mind-enclosure to the "things themselves" – still, Husserl could not fully appreciate the proper character of the "things themselves" because he continued to address what we encounter from within the framework of a modern "subjecticity," that is, principally and primarily from the side of the conscious subject. Heidegger's discomfort with this view is evident as far back as his 1919 lecture course given at Freiburg during the "war emergency semester," in which he began to take his distance from Husserl's phenomenological approach.[4] Here Heidegger criticizes Husserl's reflective, theoretical phenomenology for addressing the things we encounter as inert objects appearing for and before the sense-giving I or I-pole.

For Heidegger, though, what we encounter, what "there is" (*es gibt*), has the character of an "*Ereignis*," a "happening" or "event" within lived experience (here he employs his signature term *Ereignis* for one of the first times). In other words, things "happen" to us and address us; they are "events" of showing that we appropriate in language. As he puts it, "*es weltet*" – that is, the surrounding world "worlds"; things "world" "everywhere and always." I suggest that with this expression "*es weltet*," Heidegger was tapping into the meaning of the old verb form *welten*, "to world," which, even more evidently in English, once conveyed "to furnish and fill up" and also "to come into existence."[5] In other words, "things" *emerge and abound* about us in their eventfulness. The key point is that in his reflections here, we detect that Heidegger, very early on, was animated and guided by an exceptionally vivid sense of how things are manifest to us in an "eventful" way, how they address us and even "speak" to us, as it were. Especially notable is the poetic example he gives from Sophocles's *Antigone* of just such a vibrant, resonant "happening" in our lived experience – the splendor of the rising and shining sun. This is a perfect prefiguring of his reading in subsequent years of *phainomenon* in terms of *phainesthai* in terms of *phos* – light. Things "shining-forth" – emergence, manifestness.[6] Thus even as early as 1919, we can discern – there is this clue – that what truly interested and moved Heidegger was not so much that things are *made-present* by us (Husserl) as that things *present themselves* to us.

II. Being Is Truth in the First Place

Yet it was Heidegger's study of Aristotle in those early years, culminating in his elucidation of *Metaphysics, Theta* 10 on the *on hos alethes* – "the being *as true*," that is, "truth" as belonging most properly (*kyriotaton*) to the being itself – that confirmed his insight that to renew the question of Being was to recover the experience of Being as manifestive, as showing itself from itself, as unconcealing, as shining-forth, as opening and offering itself, as addressing us and claiming us. This is the "meaning" of Being that Heidegger sought, even if originally this seeking worked

itself out largely within an Husserlian phenomenological framework. Nonetheless, even in those early "phenomenological"
years, the word "meaning" in the formulation "the meaning of
Being" arguably served more as an indicator, a pointer, a marker
for his primary concern with the "manifestness" of Being in
relation to Dasein. Or that is certainly how the later Heidegger
understood it. In 1946, in remarks to Jean Beaufret under the
title "The Fundamental Question Concerning Being Itself" ("*Die
Grundfrage nach dem Sein selbst*"), Heidegger insisted, "With that
question [concerning Being], I have always – and from the very
beginning – remained outside the philosophical position of Husserl, in the sense of a transcendental philosophy of consciousness."[7] This is a most telling comment, and I do not think it is
meant disparagingly at all; it is simply Heidegger's realization
some years later that what he had his eye on from the outset was
very different from Husserl. That is, while Husserl was primarily
concerned with clarifying the activity of making-manifest from
the side of consciousness, he had been chiefly concerned with
Being *qua* manifestation insofar as Being makes manifest Dasein
in the first place, along with its constitutive activity of making-
manifest.

Some years later, in Le Thor in 1969, he explained further that
already in *Being and Time*, "meaning" (*Sinn*) did not have for him
the significance of "meaning" or "sense" as Husserl understood
this in terms of "sense-giving" (*Sinngebung*) acts of consciousness. He added: "*Being and Time* does not attempt to present a
new meaning of Being [understood in this Husserlian manner],
but rather to open a hearing for the word of Being – to let this
hearing be claimed by Being. In order to *be* the '*Da*,' it is a matter
of becoming claimed by Being."[8] Also at Le Thor, he emphasized
to the seminar members that in *Being and Time*, "meaning" (*Sinn*)
was never intended to refer simply to a "human performance"
(*menschliche Leistung*; *Leistung*, of course, is one of Husserl's key-
words) and thus only to the "structure of subjectivity." Rather,
"meaning" is to be explained from the "region of projection,"
which in turn is explained by "understanding" (*Verständnis*),
which itself is to be understood only in the originary sense of
"*Vorstehen*," that is, "'standing before,' residing before, holding

oneself at an equal height with what one finds before oneself, and being strong enough to abide it."'[9] In other words, his crucial point is that "meaning" must be understood most properly, that is, in the first place, as a *response* to Being (manifestation) by Dasein and not as a "performance" or "achievement" (*Leistung*) of transcendental subjectivity. We may capture his position this way: *only insofar as there is manifestation, emergence, is there meaning*. This is also to say that Being *qua* manifestation is structurally prior to, and the ontological condition of, any "constitution" of meaning.

Even so, his early talk about "the meaning of Being" proved to be sufficiently problematical for him that he turned to the expression "the truth of Being" (*die Wahrheit des Seins*) in the 1930s (including in *Beiträge*, where it appears as *die Wahrheit des Seyns*). This naming of the fundamental matter for thought appears in his writings for the rest of his life, but most notably in the work of the 1940s, including the brilliant lecture courses on Parmenides (1942–3) and Heraclitus (1943, 1944) and the important statements "Letter on Humanism" (1947) and "Introduction to 'What is Metaphysics?'" (1949).[10] Yet with this phrase "the truth of Being," he was indeed only drawing out more fully his own fundamental insight that had been there all along. Again, during the 1920s, he had repeatedly made the point that the proper locus of "truth" is "the being" (*das Seiende*) in its manifestness and that "we take part in the being's unconcealedness, *its truth (seine Wahrheit),*" as he put it in the lecture course "Introduction to Philosophy" from the 1928–9 winter semester. Here is another key passage from this lecture course:

> Yet the manifestness of the being in it itself [*an ihm selbst*] is made vividly clear to us if we describe this fact negatively and say: This being, as it is here in this context present-at-hand in it itself, is not concealed to us as what it indeed could be; it is in it itself unconcealed. Because it is unconcealed in it itself can we make propositions regarding it and also verify these propositions. The manifestness of the being is an unconcealedness [*Unverborgenheit*]. Unconcealedness actually means in the Greek *aletheia*, which

we customarily, but inadequately, translate as truth. True, that is, unconcealed, is the being itself, … Thus, not the statement and not the proposition regarding the being, but the being itself, is "true." Only because the being itself is true can statements regarding the being be true in a derivative sense.

In the tradition of metaphysics in the Middle Ages, there is, however, also a conception of truth – *veritas* – according to which truth belongs to the being itself, to the *ens*. One thesis reads: *omne ens est verum*, every being is true. But this statement has an altogether different meaning, namely, that every being, insofar as it is, is created by God; but insofar as it is created by God, *ens creatum*, it must be thought by God. Insofar as it is thought by God as the one who does not err and who is the absolute truth, the being is true by virtue of being thought by God. Because every being is a created being, it is a being of a kind that is true, *verum qua cogitatum a Deo* [true insofar as it is thought by God]. Therefore, this concept of the truth of the being rests on entirely different presuppositions from those in our exposition of truth.[11]

As noted earlier, on this point, Heidegger drew his inspiration from Aristotle (not Husserl) and specifically from Aristotle's *Metaphysics*, *Theta* 10 at 1051b, admittedly a difficult text to decipher, where Aristotle states that "being" is spoken of not only in terms of the categories and with respect to the potentiality and actuality of these, but also *in the most proper sense* (reading *kyriotaton*) as the "true."[12] Heidegger understands this text to be the culmination of Aristotle's teaching in *Theta* and as the completion of the discussion of "truth" in *Epsilon* 4 (1027b). In his view, Aristotelian scholars who have questioned or dismissed the significance of *Theta* 10 – Schwegler and Jaeger most notably – are simply displaying the modern philosophical habit of thinking that "truth" has nothing to do with "being" and is to be regarded only as an epistemological or logical phenomenon. Countering this modern bias, Heidegger calls *Theta* 10 "the keystone of Book *Theta*, which is itself the center of the entire *Metaphysics*," and he elaborates how in this chapter Aristotle speaks of the being as true (*on hos alethes*) as what is most proper (*kyriotaton*) to the being. That is, for Aristotle, the primary and proper locus of "truth" is the being as manifestive, as showing itself as it is. This is precisely the Aristotelian insight – and the ancient Greek experience more generally – that Heidegger thought was "forgotten" thereafter in the metaphysical tradition, including in the Middle Ages.

In an earlier lecture course during the winter semester of 1926–7, Heidegger had paid close attention to Thomas Aquinas's discussion of truth in *De Veritate*, especially *De Veritate* I, 1 and 2; and even earlier, in 1924, he had touched on the matter of *verum* in Aquinas in an exchange with Max Scheler that followed Heidegger's lecture in Cologne on Aristotle.[13] By the late 1920s, as reflected in the extended text cited above, Heidegger's criticism of Thomas appears to have taken this form: In the *De Veritate*, Aquinas understands Aristotle to maintain that the locus of truth is in thought or, more precisely, in the judgment that composes and divides. Yet more to the point, Aquinas asserts that, strictly speaking, being is true *only* insofar as being is brought into relation with thought, with the intellect, human and divine. Therefore, as Aquinas states in his *Respondeo* in I, 1, being may be said to be "manifestative" (*manifestativum*) or "shown" (*ostenditur*) *only as the consequence* of truth (the *effectum consequentem*, the effect following upon truth).[14] In other words, *manifestatio* (manifestation) and *ostentatio* (showing or display) do not belong to being itself, but only to being insofar as it is declared or displayed in the judgment. Accordingly, in the first reply, Aquinas refuses the apparent sense and force of Augustine's words that "the true is that which is" (*verum est id quod est*) and proposes that Augustine was not identifying truth with the act of being, the *actum essendi*, but rather was referring to being as the foundation (*fundamentum*) of truth – and that truth properly resides only in the judgment. For Heidegger, then, what was regrettably lost from view in Thomas's account was the Greek experience of Being as emergence, as arising, as showing itself, as displaying and declaring itself, as manifestation, as "truth." *Being as aletheia*. Or, as he also put it some years later, "*aletheia* is a name for *esse*, not for *veritas*."[15] That is, fundamentally, *aletheia* is a name for Being.

III. The Primacy of Being

The "forgottenness" of *the aletheic character of being (esse)* in Thomas's philosophy became more acute in Descartes's thinking, which rendered things as static objects for a subject, and in the subsequent unfolding of the modern philosophy of consciousness in which things took on the character of mere mental·objects or entities. For Heidegger, Husserl's treatment of "the things themselves" – no matter his teacher's important breakthrough – nonetheless retained this modern subjectist philosophical colouring. In this regard, there is another text worth noting: an observation that Heidegger made much later in his thinking, in 1965. Most readers will be familiar with his 1964 address "The End of Philosophy and the Task of Thinking," which appears in the *Basic Writings* volume. Yet not long afterwards, he delivered a similar address, this time on the occasion of a birthday celebration for the Swiss psychiatrist Ludwig Binswanger. This talk was later published in 1968 (in a Japanese translation, and not until 1984 in German) under the title "On the Question Concerning the Determination of the Matter for Thinking."[16] In some respects, I consider this address to be a more substantive and significant statement of his later thinking than the slightly earlier and much better-known lecture. Nevertheless to the point, Heidegger makes an observation that restates and reaffirms in yet one more way his long-standing position – the position I have been laying out here – that it is the manifestness (the truth) of the being, first brought to light by the ancient Greeks, that must again command our attention so that we may break through the immanentism of the modern philosophy of consciousness. He invites us to think back to Homer:

> We may recall a scene during the homecoming of Odysseus. With the departure of Eumaeus, Athena appears in the form of a beautiful young woman. The goddess appears to Odysseus. But his son Telemachus does not see her, and the poet says: *ou gar pos pantessi theoi phainontai enargeis (Odyssey* XVI, 161). "For the gods do not appear to everyone *enargeis*" – this word is usually translated as "visible." Yet *argos* means gleaming [*glänzend*]. What gleams, shines forth from itself. What shines forth thus, presences

forth from itself. Odysseus and Telemachus see the same woman. But Odysseus perceives the presencing of the goddess. Later, the Romans translated *enargeia*, the shining-forth-from-itself, with *evidentia*; *evideri* means to become visible to someone. Evidence is thought in terms of the human being as the one who sees. In contrast, *enargeia* is a feature of presencing things themselves.[17]

The basic complaint is a familiar one. The later Greek and Roman thinkers subtly shifted the philosophical focus away from being towards the human being as perceiver and knower. Furthermore, it was Descartes who decisively moved the human subject as the *ego cogito* to the centre of philosophical reflection. Yet in Heidegger's critical remark on "evidence" (*Evidenz*), we also hear once again, I think, a distancing from Husserl's position. Evidence, the principle of evidence, evidencing the truth – the "achievement" of transcendental subjectivity in "constituting" the "phenomenon" and in presenting such intelligible objects – this is the language of Husserl's phenomenological project that for Heidegger revealed his teacher's inability to break free and clear of the ego-subjectism of the Cartesian tradition of thinking. In other words, Husserl's call "to return to the things themselves" was a promise unfulfilled or at least only partly fulfilled. What remained of pre-eminent importance to Husserl (and, it seems, to many recent Heidegger commentators as well) was a consideration of the *noetic* or *apophantic* pole of the presentation of things – and what remained unarticulated and unaccounted for, and certainly unappreciated *as such*, was the "gleaming" of the being (*das Seiende*) itself, the "truth of the being itself."[18] Furthermore, in one of the few instances where Heidegger mentions Wittgenstein, he levels a similar but even harsher criticism. In Le Thor in 1969, he characterizes Wittgenstein's first proposition from the *Tractatus*, "The real is what is the case" (as Heidegger rendered it), as "truly an eerie [*gespenstischer*] statement."[19] He understands Wittgenstein's proposition to mean that a being is no more than "that which comes under a determination, is fixed [in signification], the determinable," and such a formulation is for Heidegger an "eerie" testament to how utterly and profoundly removed our contemporary philosophical thinking about beings is from the Greek experience of beings – the island in the sea, the mountain on the land – "leaping into view" (*springt ins Auge*) as *ta phainomena* as *ta alethea* – as "what lets itself be seen," the emerging, the manifest, the true.

Thus, to pick up the thread of the narrative I am unfolding, Heidegger had a very early insight into "the truth of *the being*," and it is, in part, *this* insight that moved him and guided him along his path of thinking during the 1920s into the famous "turn" in his thinking (*die Kehre*) after *Being and Time*, and then through the "turn" to his reformulation of *die Sache selbst* as "the truth of *Being*" in the 1930s. The expression "the truth of Being" simply made explicit what was implicit or liminal in his earlier phrase "the meaning of Being," namely, that the focal point of his thinking was, again, in his words, "*the manifestness of Being and its relation to the human being.*"[20]

The core matter therefore: "Unconcealedness-manifestation" (Being) in "relation" to "disclosedness" (Dasein) – this oneness that is two-together or this one-together with two distinct and irreducible "sides" – and in this "relation" of Being and Dasein, the structural priority or antecedence *belongs to Being*. In fact, in a seminar in 1941–2, he states clearly and decisively the matter of the irreducibility of the "truth of Being" in relation to Dasein and Dasein's constitutive meaning-making: "'Truth' is 'independent' of the human being, since truth means the essencing of what is true in the sense of unconcealedness. [In the subjectivist perspective,] 'truth' is 'dependent' on the human being and caused, brought about, made, produced. *But the human being is dependent on the truth*, if truth is [properly understood as] the lighting/clearing of Beyng as Beyng's essence, since 'to depend' means: to be determined and thoroughly attuned in essence (but not caused)."[21] In addition, in the same seminar he clarifies that manifestation and reserve belong to Being in the first place:

Manifestation is not the fruit of cognition and thus not of the same origin of essence as cognition. The concealed and likewise the unconcealed, that which is manifest, reside in Being [*sind beheimatet im Sein*].[22]

Indeed, the motif of the primacy and irreducibility of "the truth of Being" in relation to the human being's meaning-making structure is ever present in the thinking of the middle and later Heidegger and is articulated in various ways. For example, in his "Three in Conversation on a Country Path," composed 1944–5, the "teacher" or "guide" (*der Weise*) puts the matter this way: "the essence of the human being is therefore released into the regioning [*die Gegnet*] and accordingly needed by it, and solely because *the human being by himself has no power over truth, which remains independent of him. Truth can only therefore essentially unfold independently of the human being*, because the essence of the human being as releasement to the regioning is needed by the regioning ... The independence of truth *from* the human is evidently then a relation *to* the human."[23]

In the 1956 lecture course on "The Principle of Ground," he characterized the matter more succinctly: "For we are never the ones who we are apart from the claim of Being."[24] And in Le Thor in 1969, he gave clear testimony to the development of his thinking, namely, to "the turn" (*die Kehre*) in thinking after *Being and Time*:

> The thinking that proceeds from *Being and Time*, in that it gives up the phrase "meaning of Being" in favor of "truth of Being," henceforth emphasizes the openness of Being itself rather than the openness of Dasein with respect to the openness of Being. This indicates "the turn" [*die Kehre*], in which thinking always more decisively turns to Being as Being.[25]

To be sure, for Heidegger it is the case that the human being is the "shepherd of Being," "the guardian of Being." That is, we are always reminded that our access to Being is only through our Dasein – and for this reason it may be fair to say that his thinking remained broadly "phenomenological" to the end – but if so, his *enrichment* of phenomenology lay precisely in his giving a full accounting of the "phenomenon," of the "claim of Being," on the human being and our meaning-making. Nevertheless, Being itself as "ever-living" emergence became of such overriding concern to Heidegger that he sometimes explicitly stated that the "truth-ing of Being" not only *exceeds* the relation to the human being (as already noted) but is also *altogether independent* of that relation. All such statements are often overlooked and need to be taken into account – especially by those commentators who would read him in a strict transcendental-phenomenological manner:

> At times, Being needs the essencing of human being, and yet Being *is never dependent* upon existing humanity.

> The history of Being is neither the history of the human being and of a humanity, nor the history of the human relation to beings and to Being. The history of Being is Being itself, and only this.

> ... Being and the truth of Being is essentially beyond all human beings and every [historical] humanity.

> ... Being always and everywhere endlessly exceeds all beings and juts forth into beings.

> *Physis* [as Being itself] is beyond the gods and human beings.[26]

Heidegger's original and sustaining concern was with Being as manifestation as shining-forth as *phainesthai* – the spontaneous and ungrounded temporal emerging and appearing of all beings. We might also recall in this respect his fondness for quoting Angelus Silesius's poetic line: "The rose is without why; it blooms because it blooms."[27] Therefore over the years, guided especially by Aristotle's insight into the *kinetic* character of things, he unfolded his understanding of *Being itself* (*Sein selbst*) – that is, the fundamental, unifying, and originary meaning of Being – as the *Being-way*, as I prefer to name it, wherein and whereby beings emerge, linger in their "full look" or "presence" (*eidos*), wane, and pass away. As he saw it, Plato, and particularly Aristotle, remained close to this originary Greek experience of Being; in other words, the "full look," the *eidos* or *morphe* that Plato and Aristotle determined to be the *ontos on*, the "really real," represented only a *separating out and privileging* of this *one aspect* of the whole arc of presencing that is Being itself. Consequently, for Heidegger, the temporal-spatial emerging of beings in their beingness was still in the background of Plato's and Aristotle's thinking, unlike in the later metaphysical tradition in which the variations on the formulation "being itself = essence (that is, constant presence)" simply became philosophical formula.[28]

If the question is whether Heidegger himself withdrew or abandoned the name Being in speaking about his core concern – a question that has been raised by some Heidegger scholars more recently – then I have maintained that the textual evidence is compelling and convincing that he did not.[29] Moreover, if we hew close to this question, we uncover this engaging story of how Heidegger struggled mightily from beginning to end to retain the name of Being while distinguishing it from metaphysical "being(ness)." His perseverance in this effort is simply remarkable – and a measure of how important it remained to him to safeguard the originary word of Western philosophical thinking – Being – right to the very end of his lifetime of thinking. For Heidegger, there is no "beyond Being," only a "beyond being(ness)." Indeed, this is precisely how he read Plato's well-known phrase *epekeina tes ousias* from Bk VI of the *Republic*; that is, Plato was pointing beyond the Ideas, "beyond beingness," to a realm that "enables" and "empowers" the Ideas in the first place, a realm that Heidegger identified as Being itself, the temporal-spatial Being-way.[30]

This said, however, Heidegger surely enjoyed the *Spielraum*, the "free-play" or "leeway," of a thinker to name the *Ur*-phenomenon in a multitude of different ways. The many names he put into play, from the ancient Greek words *aletheia*, *physis*, *Logos* to his own terms *Ereignis*, *Lichtung*, *Gegnet*, *Es gibt*, all attempt to say and show in its several dimensions the one fundamental matter – what he properly named Beyng (*Seyn*), Being itself (*Sein selbst*), Being as such (*Sein als solches*), Being as Being (*Sein als Sein*). "Saying" (*sagen*) is ultimately a "showing" (*zeigen*), but it is also a "playing" (*spielen*), and Heidegger revelled in this "play" of saying and naming – indeed, we may imagine, as he walked the forest paths or gazed out the window of his study, meditating on how he might bring "it" into language yet one more time.

IV. Being as *Ereignis*

Let us consider further: How do Heidegger's terms of art, *Ereignis* and *Lichtung*, relate to "the truth of Being"?[31] As noted earlier, he employed the term *Ereignis* very early on in his 1919 lecture course and in a few places thereafter, but by his own testimony, it was in the years 1936–8, during which he composed the private manuscript we know as *Beiträge zur Philosophie (Vom Ereignis)* (*Contributions to Philosophy [From Ereignis]*), that he became intensely concerned with working out this notion anew, specifically in historical terms. It is well known that Heidegger never thought this dense and difficult private manuscript to be publishable, and it was not published in the *Gesamtausgabe* during his lifetime – not until 1989, in fact. *Beiträge* deserves the kind of careful attention that it has received in recent years. Even so, in my view, since its publication, the Heidegger scholarship has generally tended to overstate the significance of this one text – and to overstate, in particular, the significance of the term *Ereignis* in his thinking as a whole.

Indeed, it was not until the late 1950s and early 1960s that Heidegger presented his notion of *Ereignis* in a more direct and public way. Yet as I noted in *Engaging Heidegger*, his discussion of *Ereignis* in his later work is much more serene than in *Beiträge* and the *Beiträge*-related reflections of the late 1930s, all of which are marked by a somewhat disturbing quasi-apocalyptic tone. In his later statements, he no longer speaks of *Ereignis* in terms of the dramatic – and even traumatic – moment-ousness or event-fulness of history, but rather now as the "most gentle of all laws" that gathers each being into what it properly is and into a belonging with other beings – a characterization that is remarkably similar to his earlier descriptions of Being as the primordial *Logos* as the primordial foregathering (*Versammlung*). What is more, this characterization is remarkably in tune with his earliest use of the word *Ereignis* in the 1919 lecture course.[32]

The later Heidegger ultimately found in the word *Ereignis* a way of bringing forth in a particularly vivid way the manifold features of Being itself. From the beginning of his path of thinking, he was concerned to "ground" the metaphysical tradition's core concern with "being(ness)" by bringing into view Being as *time* – the movement, the way, in which, by which, through which beings emerge, abide in their "full look," decline, and depart. The word *Ereignis* makes manifest the Being-way by virtue of the three fundamental resonances of the word itself, namely, (1) the "event" or "happening" that is the efflorescence and effulgence of beings coming into (2) their "own" (the *eigen* of *ereignen*) and thereby (3) coming out into "full view" to Dasein (*ereignen*, related to *eräugnen*, literally "to come before the eyes," from the German word for "eye," *Auge*). This *Ereignis* of beings, this unfolding process, Heidegger referred to as the *singulare tantum* in the late 1950s[33] – the "singular as such," a phrase that no more than reiterated his frequent characterization of Being itself as the "the one," *to hen* (Greek), *das Eine;* or as "the one and only," *das Einzig-Eine.* This "singular" unfolding of beings bears within it a dimension of reserve, but just in case this might be overlooked, he sometimes had recourse to pair *Ereignis* with the word *Enteignis* as a reminder. Nevertheless, in the later work *Ereignis* conveys the simple and quiet but also profound and astonishing "coming to pass" of all things, such as the plum or cherry tree coming into luxuriant bloom – eventfully, let us say.

One observation regarding his well-known but often misread 1962 lecture "Time and Being" will help clarify the matter. Near the end of the lecture, Heidegger states: "Yet the sole aim of this lecture has been to bring into view Being itself [*Sein selbst*] as *Ereignis.*" In *Engaging Heidegger*, I commented further on this singularly important line:

> This one line would certainly be decisive and definitive were it not that he does not helpfully clarify this conclusion. He immediately shifts to a consideration of how this is *not* to be thought. That is, he warns that the "as" in this statement is especially "treacherous" because the metaphysical habit of thinking reflexively construes what follows the "as" to be only a "mode" of being(ness).

He observes that if his statement is considered in this metaphysical manner, *Ereignis* would be no more than a subset of being(ness) and therefore "subordinated" to being(ness) as "the main concept," and he emphasizes that this is certainly not his meaning. Metaphysical thinking simply misses the fundamental matter to be thought in saying "Being itself as *Ereignis*." This may be so, but he offers no careful elucidation of how his conclusion *is* to be understood, although his meaning is perhaps apparent enough that Being itself as *Ereignis* names the *giving* of beings (what-is-given) in the fullness of their givenness (*eidos*, beingness), and relatedly, the *giving* of the epochal or historical renderings of *beingness*. Yet more to the point, he does not directly address the apparent tension in the lecture between two claims: On the one hand, he states throughout that *Ereignis* "gives" *das Sein* (*Es gibt Sein*), but, on the other hand, he concludes with the strong assertion that the whole point of the lecture is precisely to bring into view "Being itself as *Ereignis*."

The problem lies with his uncertain use of the word *das Sein*. One of the chief difficulties in reading the later Heidegger is that he often leaves the reader uncertain about the meaning of *Sein* in certain contexts, and here is a particularly troublesome instance of this. Nevertheless, this is not the case with his use of the name *Sein selbst*, Being itself, because throughout his work he is always careful in reserving this name for the fundamental matter for thought. So, in "Time and Being" we find that he does not state that *Ereignis* gives or grants *Being itself*; in fact, as far as I can determine, there is *no* place in any of Heidegger's texts – early, middle, or late – where he allows that *Ereignis* gives *Being itself* (nowhere, in other words, where he uses the phrase *Es gibt Sein selbst*). Therefore, if we sort out the language of the lecture, then we can make better sense of his fundamental position: *Ereignis* as *Es gibt* gives (grants, allows, lets, enables) beingness; but *Ereignis* and Being itself say the Same.[34]

A careful consideration of "Time and Being" reveals, therefore, that there is no significant departure in Heidegger's thinking at all, but rather only a reformulation of the fundamental matter for thought in terms of *Ereignis* as *Es gibt*. Yet, moreover, let us recall that *already* in 1946–7 in the "Letter on Humanism," he had made himself perfectly clear on this point: "For the 'it' [*es*] that here 'gives' [*gibt*] is Being itself."[35] In fact, I propose that his formulation of the *Es gibt* in "Time and Being" may be regarded as a later retrieval and restatement of his very early observation on the lived-experience of the "*es gibt*" ("there is" something) as an *Ereignis* in §13–14 of the 1919 lecture course, which I highlighted at the outset of the chapter. Accordingly, I think it is possible to say that Heidegger's thinking and language in 1962 had returned to where it had essentially begun in 1919. Even so, my overarching point is that the task for thinking called for in "Time and Being" remained what it had always been, namely, to get into full view what earlier Western philosophical thinking had caught sight of only glancingly, if at all: the pure appropriating – putting into place, giving, granting, letting – of what appears (beings) in the fullness of appearing (beingness).

V. Being as *Lichtung*

Another *term d'art*, *die Lichtung*, has received little careful scholarly attention, which I have attempted to address and redress in *Engaging Heidegger*.[36] There are a number of issues to be observed, but the matter that I would focus on at present is that *die Lichtung*, variously translated as the "lighting" or as the "clearing" depending upon the period in which we find the term in Heidegger's writings, is but another name for Being itself. Surprisingly, there appears to be considerable confusion concerning this issue in the recent scholarship; some commentators continue to insist on identifying *die Lichtung* exclusively with Dasein's disclosedness or constitutive disclosive activity, and their position rests primarily on their reading of §28 of *Being and Time*. Nevertheless, by the time Heidegger wrote the "Letter on Humanism" to Jean Beaufret in 1946, he had already made it clear that precisely this kind of reading was not tenable. "But *die Lichtung* itself is Being," he pointedly stated in the "Letter."[37] Some years later, in the 1965 address in honour of Binswanger that I have cited, he came back to this matter and clarified the development of his thinking in a remarkably forthright way:

Thus it may be appropriate at this time to indicate, at least broadly, the clearing [*Lichtung*] as the distinctive matter for another thinking. This is called for because four decades ago the hermeneutic analytic of Dasein spoke about the clearing, with the aim of unfolding the question of Being in *Being and Time* ... Yet it required a decades-long walk along those forest paths that lead only so far [*Holzwege*] to realize that the sentence in *Being and Time*: "The Dasein of the human being is itself the clearing" (§28), perhaps surmised the matter for thinking but in no way considered the matter adequately, that is, in no way posed the matter as a question that arrived at the matter. The Dasein is the clearing for presence as such, and yet Dasein is, at the same time, certainly not the clearing insofar as the clearing is Dasein in the first place, that is, insofar as the clearing grants Dasein as such.[38]

His reflection here is a superb example of a *retractatio* of the Augustinian kind, not a "retraction" as such but a reworking, restating, refocusing of an earlier position. Heidegger tells us that what he could not say *quite yet* in *Being and Time* was that although Dasein is the clearing in one sense, it is not the clearing *as such*. In other words, while Dasein's disclosure (that is, "clearing") of what is must always be acknowledged and kept in view, the focal point of his thinking had always been the "clearing itself" (that is, Being itself), which "clears" or "grants" Dasein and all beings in the first place. In a conversation with Medard Boss in these same years, he made this very point even more clearly and firmly using the more familiar language of earlier writings: the human being is "the guardian of the clearing" (cf. "the guardian of Being") and "the shepherd of the clearing" (cf. "the shepherd of Being"), and as such,

the human being is not the clearing itself, is not the whole clearing, is not identical with the whole clearing as such.[39]

What is more, as late as 1973, in a seminar in Zähringen, he stated this position once again and once more in no uncertain terms:

This clearing [*Lichtung*] … this free dimension is not the creation of the human being; it is not the human being. On the contrary, it is that which is assigned to him, since it is addressed to him: it is that which is dispensed to him.[40]

In Heidegger's universe of indications: Being itself, *Ereignis*, *Lichtung* – the Same. Precisely in the same way that, according to Heidegger, "*Aletheia, Physis, Logos* are *the Same* [his italics] … as the originary self-gathering-together in the One that is rich with distinction: *to Hen*. The *Hen*, the primordially unifying One and Only, is the *Logos* as *Aletheia* as *Physis*."[41]

In summary, Being itself is the unconcealing of beings (*aletheia*); the emerging, arising, appearing, shining forth of beings (*physis*); the laying out and fore-gathering of beings (the primordial *Logos*) – but also the "appropriating" (*Ereignis*) of beings and the "lighting" and "clearing" (*Lichtung*) of beings. Yet to be more precise, characterizing Being itself as the appearing or manifesting of beings does not in the first place refer to the sheer, abiding "appearance" or "presence" of beings (which came to be spoken of in the metaphysical tradition as *eidos, morphe, ousia, energeia, actualitas, essentia*), but rather to *anwesen selbst*, presencing itself, or to "*Bewegtheit*" (Heidegger's translation of Aristotle's *kinesis*), namely, the "movedness" of all beings into and out of presence, which Heidegger meditated on at length, especially in his commentary on Aristotle's *Physics*, B I.[42] Being itself: the unifying one and only, temporal-spatial *emerging or appropriating of beings into presence* – but also the giving, granting, freeing, letting of beings – as long as we understand by "letting" this "enabling" (*Ermöchlichung*) and "empowering" (*Ermächtigung*) movement into (and out of) presence.

Concluding Thought

Truth of Being: Being *truths*. The "strangeness" of this matter for thinking was not lost upon Heidegger himself, who commented in the 1943 lecture course on Heraclitus:

> The thinking of metaphysics knows truth only as a feature of cognition. That is why the hint presently given – that "truth," in the sense

of *aletheia*, is the inception of the essence of *physis* itself and of the divinities and humans belonging therein – remains strange in every respect for all previous thinking. Yes, it is even good and crucial that we hold fast to this strange matter and not be persuaded hastily that *aletheia* is not, as metaphysics up until now has meant in a "self-evident" manner, a mere feature of cognitive comportment – but rather is the fundamental feature of Being itself. It remains strange for us and must remain strange that truth is the originary essence of Being.[43]

Several decades later, this "strange" matter for thinking continues to be largely eschewed by Continental and analytic philosophers alike – and, perhaps much more surprisingly, by many Heidegger commentators as well. Yet the way remains open for us to take up and take to heart this marvellous matter of *the truth of Being* – Heidegger's distinctive way of calling us back to the experience of Being as manifestation; to the experience of things as they emerge and meet us and, as we say in English, "fill our senses"; to the experience of ourselves "vibrating back" from things, as Walt Whitman put it. The nearness and freshness and vividness of what is, and the astonishment and joy and thanksgiving that this calls forth in us. The dynamism of all things, both made and found, both of the exuberant city and of the serene wooded path, *all beings and things* as they emerge and linger in their appearance – but also wane, falter, and pass away. There is for us to discern, too, the deep reserve inherent in the showing of things, the *lethe* dimension of *aletheia* that Heidegger spoke of so often. *Lethe*, this unconquerable reserve of Being that keeps us unsure and unknowing – and humbly *reserved* in our telling to ourselves and to others of what is. With these observations taken together, we are in view again of the core matter of Heidegger's thinking, and once more I call upon Walt Whitman to help us say this matter. In Whitman's strong voice:

A song of the rolling earth, and of words according,
Were you thinking that those were the words, those upright lines?
    those curves, angles, dots?

No, those are not the words, the substantial words are in the
ground and sea, they are in the air ...[44]

All things rolling into manifestation. All things rolling into and
out of presence. All things rolling and gathering into language.[45]
This is the "well-rounded, never trembling heart of truth" – and
the very heart of Heidegger's meditative thinking.[46]

Chapter 2

On Hölderlin on "Nature's Gleaming"

And in this way, accordingly, is Nature 'divine.'
>   From Heidegger's commentary

Primordially emerging Nature . . . appears [to the poet] in a special light.
>   Heidegger, "Hölderlin's Earth and Heaven," 1959

Sometime "after July 1970," Heidegger composed a brief but bright reflection on several of Hölderlin's so-called "last poems."[1] The principal poem considered bears the title "Autumn" and opens with the line, "Nature's gleaming is higher revealing." The complete poem reads:

Nature's gleaming is higher revealing,
Where with many joys the day draws to an end,
It is the year that completes itself in resplendence,
Where fruit come together with beaming radiance.

Earth's orb is thus adorned, and rarely clamors
Sound through the open field, the sun warms
The day of autumn mildly, the fields lie
As a great wide view, the breezes blow

Through boughs and branches, rustling gladly,
When then already to emptiness the fields give way.

The whole meaning of this bright image lives
As an image, golden splendor hovering all about.

During the 1960s, Heidegger had commended this poem to others, and it had apparently become a favourite of his.[2] This is not at all surprising because, as I would like to illuminate here, Heidegger, nearing the end of his life, had come to find in this particular poem a fitting "saying" of what he considered to be the fundamental matter (*die Sache selbst*) of his lifetime of thinking.

After setting out the poem in full, Heidegger reflects that Hölderlin composed these lines one year before his death, which "brought to an end the long period of the dark night [*Umnachtung*], a night [*Nacht*] replete with mystery, a nighting [*Nachten*] that grants such saying" (205). It is clear that Heidegger considered Hölderlin's "madness" as a kind of "divine madness" and not as a mere mental "derangement." In the "dark night" of his later years, Hölderlin could see what others could not, and, therefore, his "last poems" are capable of awakening us to "the astonishing" and to the wonder of "the extraordinary in the ordinary." Heidegger agrees with Norbert von Hellingrath's observation that there is a remarkable "clarity and dignity" to the language that speaks in Hölderlin's last poems. Only by "proceeding with this insight," Heidegger adds, can there be success in the effort "to properly hear and thoughtfully interpret Hölderlin's last poetizing."

Thus he begins by addressing the first line of the poem: "Nature's gleaming is higher revealing." Before continuing, let us pause a moment to consider our translation of this line. The German reads, "*Das Glänzen der Natur ist höheres Erscheinen.*" *Das Glänzen* is a favourite word of Hölderlin's and of Heidegger's, as will become more evident in what follows, but oftentimes this word is translated into English simply as "shining." Yet this is inadequate. *Das Glänzen* requires a more striking translation, and English obliges with a number of alliterative words that carry forward both the form of the German word and its distinctive sense: *gleaming, glistening, glimmering, glittering, glowing.* Nature does not just "shine," it "*gleams.*" Furthermore, note that this "gleaming" is a *"höheres Erscheinen,"* a "higher appearing" or a "higher revealing." "Appearing" for *Erscheinen* is perfectly suitable, but the German word also suggests something more elevated, sublime, and "holy," and for this reason, "revealing" seems to be the better choice. Even so, for now the key matter is this: Nature's distinctive "gleaming" is a *manifestation*, indeed, a "higher" kind of manifestation. But what exactly does this mean? We must follow Heidegger's reading further.

Considering more closely the phrase "nature's gleaming," he observes that "we think of nature outside, the landscape," and he cites a few lines from Hölderlin's poem "The Stroll" *("Der Spaziergang")*:

You lovely images in the valley,
Such as gardens and tree,
And then the footbridge, the narrow,
The stream barely seen,
How beautiful from bright distance
Gleams to the eye the glorious image
Of the landscape ...

These images of the landscape are resplendent, but Heidegger cautions us: "Yet the landscape is not yet nature itself. Landscape, gathered around human beings and inclined toward them, indeed lets appear nature in an initial gleaming" (206). Note the distinction: the "landscape" *(Landschaft)* is not "nature itself" *(Natur selbst)*. What Heidegger is articulating here should be very familiar to us; it is another saying of the "ontological difference" between beings and Being itself! For some reason, some recent Heidegger scholars have presumed that the later Heidegger abandoned his earlier guiding notion of the "ontological difference." Certainly, he became wary of the *expression* over time because he found that he could not fully free it from traditional philosophical thinking, but the *matter* of the "difference" between Being and beings remained fundamental to his thinking to the very end. It may be true that in later years he became troubled that the "ontological difference" – this particular naming of the matter – came to be misconstrued as referring to the traditional metaphysical "difference" between a concretely existing entity and its "essence" (between a "being" and its "beingness") or, in the language of the modern philosophy of the subject, between an "object" and its "objectiveness." Indeed, he readily admitted in later reflections that all previous Western philosophy had recognized and thematized in one way or another a "difference," but he insisted that this was no more than a derivative "difference," a difference in the realm of "beings," and not the primordial and fundamental *Differenz* (*Unterschied, Unter-Schied*) between Being – the temporal letting, giving, granting way itself – and beings, that is, all that issues forth from out of the Being-way.[3]

Accordingly, we should not be surprised that in this very late (1970 or after) elucidation of Hölderlin's poem, Heidegger in effect restates and reaffirms his long-standing consideration of the matter of the "ontological difference" by making the distinction between "nature" and "landscape." Nature, "in an initial gleaming," lets shine forth everything that belongs to the landscape. He cites a few lines from Hölderlin's poem "The Merry Life" (*"Das fröliche Leben"*) to make this same point:

Fairest landscape! where the road
Makes its way evenly through the middle,
Where the moon, the pale, rises,
When the evening wind comes up,
Where nature very simple ...

He draws our attention especially to the last line and observes: "The landscape with the multiplicity of its images can let appear 'simple nature' only because the landscape gleams from out of nature, which, as the 'simple,' is of divine essence" (206). Thus: "Nature" is the "simple," the "very simple," which allows to come-to-presence all that is present in "the landscape." Nature is the one and simple *way* whereby all things come-to-presence, and, as such, "is of divine essence"; that is, it is the "holy," if we recall one of Heidegger's favoured names for Being drawn from his earlier readings of Hölderlin's poetry. Furthermore, to underscore this theme of how the "divine" One (*hen*, Being, Nature) allows All (*panta*, beings, the multitude of things of the landscape), he cites several lines from Hölderlin's poem "Contentment" ("*Die Zufriedenheit*"):

> The tree that flourishes, the crown of branches,
> The flowers that ring the bark of the trunk,
> Are from divine nature, they are one life,
> Because above this heaven's breezes lean their way.

Crystallizing his point, he states: "In the look of the landscape, which nature grants, the gleaming of nature is: 'higher revealing.'" In other words, the untold abundance of luminous "images" of the landscape show themselves to us; they shine forth to us; they open to us and address us – but that *wherein and whereby* everything is manifest to us is Nature (Being). Furthermore, this allowing, letting, giving, granting of beings that is Nature (Being) is *itself* manifest to us in a unique way – it is precisely the *higher* revealing (appearing, manifesting) that is glimpsed and named by Hölderlin in the poem. Hölderlin also speaks in these lines of "heaven's breezes" *leaning* (*sich neigen*) towards all things, with the suggestion of their *bending* in a concernful, sheltering, sparing, protecting way towards all that is. This is the language of the poet's "last poems" that resonated so powerfully with the later Heidegger, that is, the language of Nature (*physis*, Being) *inclined* towards us, towards all things, in a gesture of gentle nurturing and preserving. One could well argue, as I would, that just this perspective is what is so compelling and attractive in the later Heidegger's thinking about Being. Nonetheless, at the very least, we should take note that long gone in such later reflections is his early view – perhaps a view to be expected of a younger man? – that "anxiety" and "strife" are constitutive of the relation between Being and Dasein.[4]

Heidegger's commentary turns to the matter of *time*, which remained central to his thinking to the end:

> The manifold of images in the manifold of seasons is pervaded throughout by the onefold of the year. The gleaming of nature lets appear the passage of the seasons. The gleaming of nature is not a state but a happening. In the passage of the seasons the year

completes itself. Even so, this passage is not the mere one-after-the-other of the times of the year. Rather, in each season the other seasons appear, pointing-ahead and pointing-back, as they interchange with one another. The gleaming of nature is a revealing in which ever already the whole of the year shines throughout and thus constantly anticipates the individual times of the year. In this manner, the "higher" of the gleaming revealing shows itself, that is, what is peculiar and proper to nature shows itself. (207)

The first two lines recall for us again Heidegger's earlier renderings of Heraclitus's saying of the *hen-panta* as "One is All."[5] That is, the One (Nature, Being) lets be and gathers together All (beings, the landscape, the seasons). Yet the One that he is speaking about is not to be confused with any kind of metaphysical entity; as he makes clear, "the gleaming of nature" is not a state or condition (*Zustand*), but a *happening* (*Geschehen*). Nature (Being) is indeed temporal, dynamic, flowing, unfolding, but the temporality of Nature itself (Being itself) must not be construed simply as "the mere one-after-the-other of the times of the year."

[handwritten margin note:] deserves higher praise

We readily recognize that this critique of time as a mere succession of "moments" or "nows" goes back to *Being and Time* and to even earlier reflections of the 1920s. With these lines, Heidegger reprises one of the fundamental themes of his life's work – but it is a return within the "turn" (*die Kehre*) in his thinking. That is, although his criticism of linear time here is essentially the same as what it was in *Being and Time*, nevertheless, it is no longer a critique that proceeds from a phenomenological analysis of Dasein's fundamental temporality (*Zeitlichkeit*). Rather, his reference is to Nature itself (Being itself). Nature itself offers the evidence of – shows to us – this more elemental temporality in the way, for example, that buds appear on trees in the dead of winter in recollection of summer and in anticipation of spring. The "gleaming" of Nature itself (Being itself) "reveals" this to us: "The gleaming of nature is a revealing in which ever already the whole of the year shines throughout and thus constantly anticipates the individual times of the year." What we glean from this is that Dasein's fundamental, authentic temporality (*Zeitlichkeit*), as it was worked out in *Being and Time*, takes on a new significance. Dasein's temporality is structured as it is *only because* it is correlated to the temporality (*Temporalität*), the time-space (*Zeit-Raum*), of Being itself. Being unfolds Dasein. Being temporalizes Dasein. This is the leitmotif of the later Heidegger's thinking on time, and therein we recognize a principal effect of *die Kehre* in his thinking after *Being and Time*.

Heidegger looks to the poem "Autumn" again and seeks to better understand the character of the "higher" revealing that is announced in the first verse line. The key, he suggests, is to be found in the last two lines:

> The whole meaning of the bright image lives
> As an image, golden splendor hovering all about.

He reads these lines this way: "The 'bright image' is the shining look of the autumnally completed year. Yet the whole of this completion 'lives' as one single image that is formed, that is, shows itself to non-sensuous seeing as 'golden splendor,' which hovers about [*umschwebt*] everything and thus appears as 'the whole meaning'" (207). This explication is dense and difficult to follow, admittedly, but his meaning appears to be that Nature (the One, the Simple, Being), which unfolds the landscape (all beings), manifests itself to us in a special manner that is different from the way that discrete things are manifest to us. Nature (Being) shows itself to us, *but not as a being, not as something in the landscape*. Therefore, we "see" Nature (Being) differently from the way we "see" things. Not an ordinary seeing or perception, but a special "seeing" that glimpses the "whole" process of the unfolding of all things – the very *presencing itself* of everything. Presencing itself (Nature, Being) is a "golden splendor" that suffuses, bathes ("hovers about") everything that is. Heidegger does not mean to say, I think, that this special "seeing" is "non-sensuous" in the strict sense; rather, he wishes only to distinguish our "seeing" of Nature (Being) from our usual "seeing" of things. Once again, we can "see" Nature (Being) only because presencing itself *is manifest* to us in this special, "higher" way. Since the manifestation of Nature (Being) is unique, he can maintain, not in this particular commentary but in other statements, that Being is, relative to beings, *inapparent*.[6] But, to repeat, this means only that Being is no being (Nature is not the landscape); Being is the No-thing that nonetheless *shines out brightly* to those who can "see" in this special way.

There is no question, then, that for Heidegger, Nature (the One, the Simple, Being) manifests itself to us; it is the "higher revealing" that Hölderlin heralds. This "higher" manifestation is "gleaming" and "golden," and he observes that these are favourite words of Hölderlin's poetizing. What he does not mention, however, is that they are also favourite words of his own thinking. In the later work, there are numerous instances of his use of these words, and he had undertaken an excursus on these and related words in Pindar's *Isthmian Ode 5* in an undelivered lecture course on Anaximander that was prepared for 1942.[7] The Being-way "shines forth" in a unique manner, and the uniqueness is captured especially by the poetic words "gleaming" (*Glänzen*) and "golden" (*golden*). Hence Heidegger comments, speaking as much for himself as for Hölderlin:

> "Golden" names the highest and richest gleaming, the most luminous and most pure shining. The golden gleaming hovers about the whole, forms its wholeness, and is the completing. Nevertheless, "higher revealing" cannot be considered simply as a lacking remainder to be added on. The completing is not a supplement. Rather, it brings forth in the first place the orb of the wholeness of the whole that hovers about everything, just as a shining wreath "wreathes" everything that appears. The "higher revealing" happens in the gleaming that completes [*im ergänzenden Glänzen*]. This *is* nature – allows nature to linger as itself. And in this way, accordingly, is nature "divine." (207–8)

Nature (Being) shows itself as the gleaming "whole" that allows all beings to be and may be likened to a "shining wreath" that "wreathes everything that appears." As this radiant "orb of the wholeness of the whole," Nature (Being) is the "divine," *the holy*. Most assuredly, this does not speak to any kind of traditional onto-theology. Nonetheless, this language does reflect Heidegger's profound and abiding reverence for Nature (Being) as *physis* as the unceasing emerging, lingering, passing away of all beings and things,[8] and of his experience of the essential joy that comes with our releasement to and harmonizing with the Being-way. Nature (Being), *das Heitere*, the Bright and Joyful itself – and our *relation* to Nature (Being) – is for him the "brighter bliss" spoken of in Hölderlin's line of verse:

> When out of heaven brighter bliss
>   pours forth ...

Finally, he returns once more to the first line of the poem: "Nature's gleaming is higher revealing." He observes that, in the end, this verse line is perhaps best elucidated by Hölderlin himself through another poem of his, a very special poem because it was probably composed on the last day of his life. The title of the poem is *Die Aussicht*, "The View," and I make note that it is hardly known to English readers since no translation of it appears in any major collection of Hölderlin's poems. According to Heidegger, this poem is Hölderlin's final gift to us, and he continues:

> It opens to those who hear a view into the being [*Dasein*] of the poet, who speaks from out of the silent brightness of the dark night of his spirit that has come to rest. The poem is a lasting gift wherein the poet's glimpse of the essence shelters in the simple word the "whole meaning" of everything that appears, in order to entrust it to our language as "the view" for all who see. (208)

Heidegger presents the poem in full:

The View

When into the distance passes the dwelling life of people,
Where into the distance glimmers the time of the vines,
Comes also the empty fields of summer,
And the forest with its dark image appears.

That nature completes the image of the seasons,
That nature stays, as the seasons glide along in haste,
Is from fulfillment; then high heaven gleams
Upon the people, as trees are wreathed with blooms.[9]

Although Heidegger does not comment further on this poem, we can readily understand why he found it to be a culminating poetic statement of what he had attempted to say about the poem "Autumn." The first stanza speaks to the temporality of Nature itself wherein and whereby all things, including ourselves, sojourn. The second stanza brings his fundamental message home: "That nature stays, as the seasons glide along in haste." All that is *given* comes and goes, arrives and departs, but the *giving itself* (Nature, Being) "stays," that is, remains one, whole, simple, complete. All things flow from out of "fulfillment" (Nature-*physis*), and from out of Nature ("high heaven") there "gleams," there pours forth, upon us, "people dwelling," a wholesomeness that makes us whole and brings us into the fullness of our essencing. For the later Heidegger especially, the *gleaming, glistening, glimmering, glittering, glowing* that is the manifestness of Being to humans – the *phos* at the very core of *phainesthai* – calls forth from us wonder and astonishment and great joy; brightens, lightens, and opens us; inclines our thinking towards *thanking*; and humbles us into recognizing the limit of all our saying, language, meaning – or as the poet expressed this, cited so approvingly by Heidegger at the close of his commentary:

> Yet so very simple the images, so very holy these, that one is really often fearful of describing these.

Chapter 3

The "Greek Experience" of Nature–*Physis*–Being

That [which is marked by the word *physis*] is the *overabundance,* the *excess* of what presences.

Heidegger, *Seminar in Le Thor,* 1969

Hölderlin names Nature the Holy.

Heidegger, "As When On a Holiday ...," 1941

Thematically, there is nothing fundamentally new to be found in Heidegger's oft-mentioned lecture of 1962, "Time and Being." His focus remained on Being itself as *Ereignis* as the temporal-spatial emerging of beings in their beingness (in the ensemble) – the presencing of what is present, the pure giving of what is given. Thus he states, "Yet the sole aim of this lecture has been to bring into view Being itself [*Sein selbst*] as *Ereignis.*" Furthermore, he emphatically pointed out at the end of the lecture that everything he had said regarding *Ereignis* as *Es gibt* was not new at all, but rather "the oldest of the old in Western thought: the most ancient that conceals itself in the name *A-letheia.*" To think Being itself as *Ereignis* as *Es gibt* – "Being without beings" as he characterized it in the lecture – is also to think *Aletheia.*[1]

Nevertheless, we do detect in "Time and Being" a variation in his formulation of the fundamental matter for thought (*die Sache selbst*) that is more characteristic of his writings of the 1960s, namely, the emphasis on the "letting" character of Being itself. That Being itself is the "letting" of beings in their full look (*eidos*, beingness) was always implicitly conveyed by his earlier indications that *Sein selbst* is the emerging, arising, appearing of beings (*physis*) or the laying out and gathering of beings (the primordial *Logos*) or the presencing of beings (*das Anwesen*, in the verbal sense). In the lecture, however, Heidegger seemed to have become especially frustrated that his earlier formulations were still not understood in the proper way – as he would often say, primarily because we who are accustomed to speaking of "beings" only as static "objects" and "facts" have lost the ability to "hear" the names of Being as the Greeks heard them. Consequently, in the 1960s he often turned to the language of "letting" (*Lassen*) and "giving" (*Es gibt*) in order to counter yet again the philosophical habit of thinking only beings in their beingness or objects in their objectiveness. Being itself as the "letting" of beings says the Same as the "emerging" and "unconcealing" and "presencing" of beings – but it is the language of "letting" that, at this later point in his thinking, he found especially helpful to indicate *die Sache*.

There is confirmation for this in the seminars that Heidegger conducted later in September of that year (1962), but I think that his clearest statement can be found a few years later, in the last seminar held at Le Thor in 1969 (11 September). He begins by stating plainly that "Being lets beings come to presence," and continues:

> It is a matter here of understanding that the deepest meaning of Being is *letting* [*das Lassen*]. Letting beings be, this is the non-causal meaning of "letting" in "Time and Being." This "letting" is something fundamentally different from "doing." The text "Time and Being" attempted to think this "letting" still more fundamentally in the expression "giving." The *giving* meant here speaks in the expression *Es gibt*.[2]

He adds that his point in highlighting "letting" and "giving" is that by doing so, "it is no longer the presence [*Anwesenheit*] of a being which draws one's attention, but the ground which that being covers over [temporally-spatially] in order to make itself independent from [the ground]: thus, letting as such." In the seminar, as in "Time and Being," he was trying to find fresh language that would draw our attention *away* from what-is-present (the being, *das Seiende* as *das Anwesende*) in its sheer presence (beingness, *die Seiendheit* as *die Anwesenheit* or *das Anwesen* in the nominative, not verbal sense) in order for us to "see" pure coming-to-presence itself (*anwesen selbst*), that is, what he had referred to as "Being without beings" in "Time and Being." By focusing on "the *letting* itself," he concluded in Le Thor, "one [finally] stands before *Being as Being*" (60).

I.

In "Time and Being," Heidegger brought the language of "letting" and "giving" to the forefront, but, again, the core matter of his thinking remained the same: the movedness (*Bewegtheit*) of all things into and out of presence. It had always been his claim that if we were able to truly "hear" the Greek language, then we would be able to discern this "movedness" in the *Ur*-words *physis, Logos, hen, aletheia*. Indeed, in the *Parmenides* lecture course of 1942–3, he had put the matter perfectly clearly with regard to *physis*: "The *phuein* of *physis*, the letting come forth and the emerging, *lets* what emerges appear in the unconcealed."[3] For Heidegger, the Greeks never spoke simply of static "presence"; their experience of "presence" was dynamic, as he noted in 1965:

> What we call, ambiguously and confusedly enough, beings the Greek philosophers experienced as what-is-present [*das Anwesende*] because Being was granted to them as presence [*Anwesenheit*]. And in this [presence], what was thought together was the passage from presencing to absencing, from arriving to departing, from emerging to passing away, that is, movement.[4]

In other words, the Greek thinkers never proffered what we now so routinely refer to as a "metaphysics of presence" because they never lost sight of the *presencing* of all things, even if they could not thematize this as such. Yet in fact, it is we who are accustomed to thinking of beings as merely inert objects for a subject *and even posited by a subject* – it is we who need to be reminded of the temporal "ground" of beings that "lets" and "gives" what-is-present in its presentness. His language of "letting" and "giving" in "Time and Being" attempted to say (*sagen*) and thereby show (*zeigen*) – *in yet one more way* – what manifests itself as the inner "empowering" and "enabling" of all things, namely, *Being itself*.

Even so, well after "Time and Being," Heidegger continued to use the simple term "presence" (*Anwesenheit*) in the way that he understood the Greeks to have experienced it, as the text from 1965 cited above clearly shows. In another such instance, he wrote a heartfelt sixtieth-birthday greeting to Hannah Arendt from his Black Forest *Hütte* in October 1966. In the course of his note, he voiced to her his strong objection to how contemporary readers of his work were insistent on subjectivizing or intellectualizing his understanding of *aletheia*. He wrote that his visits to Greece

> have testified to this one thing, still hardly thought, that *A-letheia* is not a mere word and not an object for etymologizing – but the ever-prevailing power of the presence [*Anwesenheit*] of all beings and things.[5]

"*The presence of all beings and things.*" One might say that the presence of all beings and things "to us," to Dasein, is understood here (Dasein as the "shepherd" and "guardian" of Being), and on this basis, one could maintain that Heidegger's thinking remained broadly "phenomenological," as some commentators have pressed this point. Nevertheless, the *focal point* of Heidegger's thinking was the temporal self-showing of things, that is, their opening, manifestation, shining-forth to us: "It is rather Being," Heidegger stated in his 1962 Preface to William J. Richardson's book, "as presencing, marked by its time-character, that *approaches* Dasein."[6]

Being approaches Dasein, ever new, ever fresh. Dasein is – in the first place – receptive (the receiver, *der Vernehmer*) of Being *qua* manifestation (*phainesthai*), even as Dasein is also manifestive (*apophainesthai*). Put another way, the manifestness of Being is structurally prior to Dasein's manifestive activity, and this is what I refer to as the structural primacy of Being in relation to the human being.[7] Furthermore, the *presence* of things to us is never exhausted by meaning: a friend, the sea, the tree, the flower – all that present themselves to us – are always more than how we present them. Cézanne painted Mont Sainte-Victoire more than sixty times by several accounts, but never once did he think he had exhausted its showing, its manifestation. Similarly, we, in turn, can never say enough about even one of Cézanne's paintings of the mountain! All things show themselves to us and address us – again and again – and they are always more than their sense or meaning. Presence (*Anwesenheit*) always exceeds, overflows, meaning and therefore is not reducible to meaning. *Sein* is not reducible to *Sinn*.

II.

For Heidegger, *aletheia*, as a name for Being itself, speaks to the power of the presencing, the *"truthing,"* of all "beings" (*Wesen, Lebewesen,* what is living, natural) and all "things" (*Dinge,* what is crafted by humans) – altogether, *physis* in the originary, fullest, and richest sense. Being (*physis*) is the presencing of all "beings and things" together in the ensemble – the village in the valley, the barn by the pasture, the windmill in the meadow, the sailboat on the sea, the lighthouse at the shoreline, the footbridge over the stream, the steeple against the sky, the road through the woods, the stone wall along the hillside, the hut among the trees, and so forth.

These images bring to mind the rich Western tradition of "pastoral" poetry, literature, music, and art, and the later Heidegger recognized the affinity of his thinking with this tradition, which reaches back to the ancient Greeks and to the Greek poet Theocritus in particular. Heidegger's reflections on his first trip to Greece in 1962, published as *Aufenthalte* (*Sojourns*), are perhaps familiar to many, but not so his observations on a later trip (May 1967), which are gathered in a shorter piece titled "On the Islands of the Aegean" (OIA).[8] In this later philosophical travelogue, he reprises several themes from *Sojourns,* but in OIA he attends more closely to the matter of the Greek understanding of *physis.* The importance for Heidegger of the Greek *Ur*-word *physis* cannot be overstated – it remained at the heart of his lifelong effort to think the originary, unifying, and fundamental meaning of Being. We must ever endeavour, he tells us in OIA, to return to the "originary meaning of nature as *physis*" that prevailed among the ancient Greeks, and, accordingly, this means understanding Nature-*physis* as the "emerging-and-letting-come-to-presence of what is present" (260). Thereby Heidegger recalls for us once more that the Greeks experienced the power of the *emergence* of all things, the opening and showing of all things to us. As he looked upon the Greek island of Kos from aboard his ship in the Aegean, he was reminded of "the last great Greek lyric poet Theocritus," who in the *Idyll, The Harvest Festival,* "celebrated the life and beauty of nature on this island." Heidegger highlights the following lines from the last part of this *Idyll:*

Eucritus and I and pretty Amyntas turned aside
To the farm of Phrasidamus, where we sank down
With pleasure on deep-piled couches of sweet rushes,
And vine leaves freshly stripped from the bush.
Above us was the constant quiet movement of elm
And poplar, and from the cave of the Nymphs nearby
The sacred water ran with a bubbling sound as it fell.
Soot-black cicadas chattered relentlessly on
Shady branches, and the muttering of tree-frogs
Rose far off from the impenetrable thorn bush.
Larks and finches were singing, the turtle-dove moaned,
And bees hummed and darted about the springs.
Everything smelt of the rich harvest, smelt of the fruit-crop.
Apples and pears rolled all around us, enclosing
Our bodies with plenty; branches reached to the ground,
Bent with the weight of plums. Men broke for us
Four-year-old seals from the mouths of their wine jars. (269)[9]

This lovely pastoral scene clearly moved Heidegger (as it has so many others over the centuries), and he also saw in it confirmation that the Greeks enjoyed a special relation to Nature-*physis.* The Greeks did not have merely a subjective "feeling" or "sentiment" for nature, which he suggests is the prevailing characteristic of the modern Romantic relation to nature.[10] Nor did the Greeks relate to "nature" as an object for a subject, a relation that developed out of the modern scientific-technological way of thinking that was principally inaugurated by Descartes. Rather, the ancient Greeks enjoyed an *immediate* (*unmittelbar*) experience of Nature-*physis* that was unencumbered by an incessantly *mediating* "subject" – a "subjectism" or "subjecticity" that is at the foundation of the modern age. Modern Romanticism and modern science and technology only *appear* to be opposites; in fact, they are united by this underlying assumption that the foundation for *thinking and feeling* is the "self" or "subject." The ancient Greeks' relation to Nature-*physis* was not burdened or hindered in this modern manner, and they were, therefore, more transparent to the *emerging* of all things. Theocritus composed his *Idylls* while dwelling in the midst of the ever-prevailing power of Nature-*physis*.

This is the thrust of Heidegger's reflections on *physis* in his travel essay. His aim, then, in citing Theocritus is to recover for us the distinctive Greek experience of Nature-*physis*-Being. Not long after he composed OIA, he restated this basic position in a more deliberate way in the first seminar in Le Thor in 1969 (2 September). The Greeks, he told the seminar participants, "resided in the midst of phenomena," and they were radically transparent to Nature-*physis* because they did not take their bearing to *physis* from the notion of an "*ego cogito*" or "subject." At the core of their experience of *physis*

> is the *overabundance*, the *excess* of what presences. Here one should recall the anecdote of Thales: he is that person so struck by the overabundance of the world of the stars that he was compelled to direct his gaze towards the heavens *alone*. In the Greek climate, the human is so overwhelmed by the presencing of what is present, that he is compelled to the question concerning what is present *as* what is present. The Greeks name the relation to this thrust of presence *thaumazein* [wonder, astonishment].[11]

Nature-*physis*-Being is this "thrust of presence," and we are astonished before the "overflow of presence" or "excess of presence" (38, *das Übermaß der Anwesenheit*). Even in Plato and Aristotle, this remained the case, according to Heidegger, and his comment clearly affirms that Being as manifestation is prior in importance to Dasein and Dasein's meaning-making (and that there is indeed "shining-forth" apart from the human being):

> We must never allow ourselves to lose sight of the fact that the determinations of *phainesthai* and of the [*on hos*] *alethes* are fully presented in the Platonic *eidos*. One is ever tempted to hear *idein* in *idea*, whereas the outward appearance [*Aussehen*] has priority, the way and manner that the thing shows forth, and not the view that one has of it, a view that one is only able to form on the basis of what the appearance first *gives forth*. Nothing is less Greek than what Schopenhauer says of Plato (intended is the statement regarding the desert that exists only thanks to my thinking it); contrary to Schopenhauer, Aristotle says: Even if no human being were to see them, the stars would shine forth nonetheless. (40; his reference is to Aristotle, *Metaphysics* VII, 1041a)

The modern turn to the human being as the foundation for thinking and feeling transformed the essential Greek experience of Nature-*physis*. As he puts it pointedly, "The Greeks are those human beings who lived immediately [*unmittelbar*] in the manifestness of phenomena – through the specifically ek-static capacity of letting the phenomena speak to them (modern man, Cartesian man, *se solum alloquendo*, speaks only to himself)" (37). And similarly: "For the Greeks, things appear. For Kant, things appear to me" (36). In other words, for Kant, as for Husserl in his own way, what is determinative – and therefore decisive – is the human being's *construction or constitution* of appearance.

Thus his point is made, indeed. Yet he offers a related observation that is worth taking into account. He asks: "How is the experience of a being to be distinguished when it is understood as *hypokeimenon* from when it is understood as *phainomenon*?" His answer underscores once more that the Greek experience is fundamentally concerned *not* with how the human being makes-manifest, but with how things are manifest to us:

> Suppose we look upon a particular being, for example a mountain in the Lubéron. If it is taken as *hypokeimenon*, then the *hypo* names

a *kata*, more precisely the *kata* of a *legein ti kata tinos*. Of course, the Lubéron mountain does not actually disappear if it is spoken of as a *hypokeimenon*, but it no longer stands there as a *phenomenon* – no longer to be seen *as giving itself from itself. It no longer presences from itself forth.* [Rather,] as *hypokeimenon* it is *that about which* we speak. (36, my emphasis)

He adds that in pure "naming," which is the fundamental way that we human beings make manifest what is manifest, "I let what is present be what it is. Without a doubt naming includes the one who names – but what is proper to naming is precisely that the one who names only enters in *to step into the background before* the being. The being, then, is pure phenomenon" (36).

With all this in mind, let us return to Heidegger's high praise for Theocritus and pose a question. He maintains that Theocritus's poetry reflects the special relation that the ancient Greeks had to Nature-*physis*, and we have set out the basic character of this special relation. However, is Heidegger making the further claim that the Greek experience of Nature-*physis* was so singular that it has not been enjoyed by human beings since? This would be a dubious claim, especially since Heidegger himself appeared to be speaking from out of the "Greek experience" and made every effort to recover this experience for all human beings. Further, it would seem altogether evident that this kind of close and "immediate" relation to Nature-*physis* is also to be found after the Greeks, for example, in Virgil's *Eclogues*, Beethoven's *Pastoral Symphony*, Wordsworth's and Whitman's poetry, Thoreau's meditations, Thomas Cole's painting, or Ansel Adams's photography. More reasonably, then, with his appeal to "the Greek experience" (*die griechische Erfahrung*), Heidegger was principally pointing to the human being's *primordial and authentic experience of Nature-physis* and not simply to a historical people and period. In other words, we might say that the "Greek experience" is, in the first place, a structural category, an *ontological–existential* mode of existing, and not an *ontic–existentiell* historical fact. Nevertheless, I must admit a difficulty here, because Heidegger's rhetoric, or more precisely his distinctive rhetorical strategy of valorizing the ancient Greek experience, sometimes did lead him to make (or at least strongly suggest) the narrower claim that "the Greek experience" of Nature-*physis* belonged to the Greeks of history *and to them only.*

Yet it was, after all, the proper character of Nature-*physis*, as well as the proper relation of Dasein to Nature-*physis*, that most concerned him. With respect to this core matter, his view was perfectly clear, as the texts we have examined bear out: Nature-*physis* is the temporal manifestation of beings in their beingness, and Dasein dwells in the midst of this manifestness. The "Greek experience" is the counter, the foil, to our modern philosophical and psychological preoccupation with grounding everything in the "subject" – and it is the remedy as well. To recover the "Greek experience" is for us to recover the joyful wonder and astonishment at the inexhaustible giving-showing-shining-forth of all things and to accept with humility the *limit* of all our saying, language, meaning concerning what is. To the contrary of certain recent readings of Heidegger, the core matter of his thinking is not our meaning-making, as important as this is, but rather *what calls for and calls forth* meaning, namely, Nature-*physis*-Being. No matter the breadth and depth of our words and meanings, we do not – we cannot – exhaust the manifestation of Nature. The vault of the heavens, Wordsworth reminds us in the poem "A Night-Piece," endlessly "deepens its unfathomable depth." For e.e. cummings, "the mightiest meditations of mankind / cancelled are by one merely opening leaf."[12] And Hopkins affirms in these lovely lines:

And for all this, nature is never spent;
There lives the dearest freshness deep down things.[13]

Focusing on Dasein's constitutive sense-making structure or on Dasein's absorbed, everyday, skilful coping practices simply does not get to the heart of the matter of Heidegger's lifetime of thinking. Both approaches, I think it is now clear, fall short of the "Greek experience."

III.

In Heidegger's view, Johann Peter Hebel was not merely a popular poet of the people; there was a surprising – and unappreciated – depth to his poetry and writings. Like Hölderlin, Hebel could see through all that is present – in all of its lustre – to the "source" of all that is present, *presencing itself*, that is, Nature-*physis*-Being. In his essay on Hebel published in 1957 ("Hebel – Friend of the House"), Heidegger, citing Hebel's words and images, speaks about how the poet, the "friend of the house" (world, Being), "guards what is essential, to which humans as those who dwell are entrusted, yet of which they are all too easily oblivious in their slumbers."[14] Like "the moon" spoken of in Hebel's "Reflections on the World Structure," the poet "is the one who stays awake the whole night through. He watches over the right kind of rest for the dwellers; he watches out for what threatens and disturbs." Also like the moon, the poet watches over the night and "watches how boys kiss girls," yet this "observing is one of wonderment, not a curious gaping."

The poet, the friend of the world, sees and cherishes every natural and crafted thing, as well as all the doings of mortals, such as boys and girls kissing in the soft light of the night. Yet the poet at the same time sees more, sees how all of this comes to pass, the very coming-to-pass itself. The poet "gathers the world into a saying whose word remains a softly restrained shining in which the world appears as if being caught sight of for the first time," and the aim is never "to instruct or to educate" but simply to make known and let be. This is how the poet "preaches," not as a "minister" – for "the poet who preaches [as a minister] is a poor poet" – but rather as one who "lets what is to be said appear in its shining" (96).

Thus Hebel, like Hölderlin and the ancient Greek poets and thinkers, recognized that human beings dwell in the midst of manifestness and that our naming and saying, in the fundamental sense, is a cor-respondence to this manifestness. This is the welcome relief from the dominant assumption of the modern philosophy of consciousness – Husserl's included – that it is our activity of making-sense that is determinative and decisive. Yet, moreover, Hebel caught sight, too, of the very source and spring of the manifestness of all things, namely, "the naturalness of nature [*die Natürlichkeit der Natur*]," the unfolding of all things,

to which the ancient Greek thinkers once gave the name "*physis*": the rising and receding of all that is present in its presencing and absencing. The natural of nature is that rising and setting of the sun, of the moon, of the stars, which immediately [*unmittelbar*] addresses dwelling human beings, thereby commending to them the mysteriousness of the world. (97; modified)

Consequently, to return to the language of "Time and Being" with which we began this chapter, for Heidegger, what addresses us and claims us is not only the radiance of what is manifest, but also the unique shining of pure "letting" (*Lassen*) and "giving" (*Es gibt*) itself – indeed, the very "gleaming," the "higher revealing," that we highlighted in the last chapter.

Concluding Thought

What, then, is the "Greek expeience" of Nature-*physis*-Being? It is the experience of every poet, every thinker, every artist, *every human being* who has an abiding awareness of the emergence of all beings and things; who sees the hidden stream, the way, of all beings and things; who glimpses the "letting" and "giving," the lighting and clearing, of all beings and things; who is released, open, and transparent to the vivid and vibrant presence of all beings and things as they unfold. This was clearly Heidegger's experience – indeed from the very beginning – but which came to fullest expression in the later work. His lifelong effort to bring to language the "ever-prevailing power" of Nature-*physis*-Being was rigorously philosophical, to be sure, but it also attained the poetic. His life's work stands as a luminous philosophical song, a paean, to "the gleaming of Nature."

Chapter 4

The Early Saying of Being
as *Physis* (as *Aletheia*)

Then *physis* shows itself as the inception – prevailing over everything – of the human being.
                    Heidegger, "On the Islands of the Aegean," 1967[1]

A motion and a spirit [that] rolls through all things.
                    William Wordsworth, "Tintern Abbey"

Being as *physis*. Being: *physis*: the Same. I have highlighted this central position of Heidegger's lifetime of thinking in the previous chapters.[2] Yet it is important to state again, this time reaching back to his early work, and especially the work of the 1930s. In fact, this task has become quite necessary because of the recent trend in Heidegger studies, which I have noted in chapter 1, to overstate the importance of Heidegger's private, experimental reflections in *Beiträge zur Philosophie (Vom Ereignis)* (1936–8) and thereby to overlook – or push into the deep background – the principal theme of Being as *physis* as *aletheia* that he worked out so carefully and compellingly in the early writings, culminating in the 1935 lecture course *Introduction to Metaphysics*. I certainly do not deny the uniqueness of *Beiträge* – nor do I fail to recognize and appreciate the inspired scholarship it has engendered in recent years[3] – but it remains that the text is especially uneven, an outpouring of intense (often personal) reflections, judgments, terms, and formulations. *Beiträge* is important, but it is not, as some have taken it up, an *Ur*-text that gives us access to an *Ur*-Heidegger; and I propose that the time has come to return our attention to Heidegger's truly major philosophical work of the 1930s, *Introduction to Metaphysics* (IM).[4]

I. *The Fundamental Concepts of Metaphysics* (1929–30)

Heidegger's engagement in IM with the Greek understanding of *physis* emerged from earlier reflections. For the present, I would like to highlight his remarks on *physis* in two statements leading up to IM: the lecture course of 1929–30, *The Fundamental Concepts of Metaphysics: World Finitude, Solitude* (GA 29/30; hereafter FCM);[5] and the summer 1932 lecture course, only recently published in the *Gesamtausgabe* (GA 33), titled *The Beginning of Western Philosophy: Interpretation of Anaximander and Parmenides* (hereafter BWP).[6]

In FCM, in his effort to lay bare the originary meaning of "metaphysics," Heidegger turns to a discussion of the Greek understanding of *physis*. In just a few paragraphs, he lays out a characterization of *physis* that informs and defines all of his later meditations on the matter. He observes that the word "nature," which is the customary translation of *physis*, is derived from the Latin *natura-nasci*, that is, "to be born, to arise, to grow" (25:38). He admits that this is also the fundamental meaning of the Greek words *physis* and *phuein*. The "middle" and "later" Heidegger is already in evidence as he elaborates this point in FCM in a markedly poetic manner:

> We here take growth and growing, however, in the quite elementary and broad sense in which it irrupts in the primal experience of the human being: growth not only of plants and animals, their arising and passing away taken merely as an isolated process, but growth as this occurring in the midst of, and permeated by, the changing of the seasons, in the midst of the alternation of day and night, in the midst of the wandering of the stars, of storms and weather and the raging of the elements. Growing is all this taken together as one.

"Growing," in the fundamental sense, "permeates" all natural phenomena. Nevertheless, to be more precise and "closer to the originally intended sense" of *physis*, he expresses a preference for the translation "the self-forming prevailing (*Walten*) of beings as a whole."[7] Therefore, "nature" is not to be understood in the narrow way that it is understood in the natural sciences today, yet he adds that it is also not to be construed in Goethe's sense or in any other "broad, pre-scientific sense." In what sense, then? This is precisely the matter that Heidegger attempted to clarify and say again and again in the full course of his lifetime of thinking. In this text, we find his early effort to bring to language the distinctiveness of *physis*:

> Rather this *physis*, this prevailing of beings as a whole, is experienced by the human being just as immediately and entwined with things in himself and in those who are like him, those who are with him in this way. The events which the human being experiences in himself: procreation, birth, childhood, maturing, aging, death, are not events in the narrow, present-day sense of a specifically biological process of nature. Rather, they belong to the general prevailing of beings, which comprehends within itself human fate and history. (26:39)

He is seeking a characterization that will be adequate to the *Ur*-phenomenon of *physis* as he understood the ancient Greeks to have experienced it. It is evident, I think, that he is not yet in full command of his language, but in his observation that follows, we find that he is already – in 1929–30 – perfectly clear that *physis* must be considered the measure, not the human being:

> *Physis* means this whole prevailing that prevails through the human being himself, a prevailing that he does not have the power over, but which precisely prevails through and around him – him, the human being, who has always already spoken out about this. Whatever he understands – however enigmatic and obscure it may be to him in its details – he understands it; it nears him, sustains and overwhelms him as that which is. (26:39)

The significance of this passage must not be missed. Heidegger states a position that he will insist upon in one way or another for the remainder of his life: in the relation between the human being and *physis* (Being), the structural antecedence belongs to *physis* (Being). From out of *physis* all things emerge, including human beings and "even in a certain way the divine beings." Yet what is more, his observation on the relation between the human being and *physis*-Being looks forward – remarkably so – to the leitmotif of his readings of Heraclitus in 1943 and 1944, which I take up in chapters 5 and 6:

> The highest that the human being has in his power is to say what is unconcealed, and in unison with this, acting *kata physin* [in accordance with *physis*], that is, joining together with and tuning into the whole prevailing and fate of the world generally. Acting *kata physin* is fulfilled in such a manner that he who thus utters, hearkens to things. (28:42)

Later in the same discussion, he attempts to separate out "the two meanings of *physis*" (30:45) that were bound together in the Greek word from the beginning. He would repeat this effort many times in his later writings. On the one hand, *physis* indicated for the Greeks "whatever prevails," that is, what is manifest (beings) "for immediate experience," such as "the vault of the heavens, the stars, the ocean, the earth." Nevertheless, he observes, *physis* came to refer more specifically to a "region of beings," namely, natural beings, the *phusei onta*, in distinction from another region of beings governed by *techne* or human "skill, invention, and production." Even so, the Greeks sustained a deep appreciation for both *physis* and *techne* in comparison to our modern and present-day understanding. For Heraclitus and for the Greeks generally, *physis*, even in the narrower sense, was exalted as "the ever-flaming fire" that "always was, always is, and always will be" and that "neither a god nor any human being created" (31:47).

On the other hand, according to Heidegger, we can discern a "second meaning" of the ancient Greek word *physis*. The second meaning points beyond "what prevails" to "the *prevailing* of whatever prevails," "*prevailing* as such" (*Walten als solches*). With this formulation, we again recognize Heidegger's motif of the "ontological difference," that is, the fundamental and primordial "difference" between beings ("what prevails") and Being itself ("the prevailing as such"). He does not specifically use the expression "ontological difference" in this context, but the core matter for thinking is the same. Even so, in this part of the lecture course he is more concerned to sketch out the particular historical Western philosophical development of this second meaning of *physis*. In other words, from the very beginning among the Greeks, *physis* referred not only to "what prevails" in manifestation but also to the prevailing or manifesting itself. Yet how was the "prevailing as such" addressed in subsequent philosophical thinking? This leads him to a discussion of how in Aristotle "the prevailing of what prevails" became "that which makes beings beings," namely, *ousia* (perduring presence; the being-ness of beings) (33:50). In this way, then, Aristotle took a decisive step towards the development of the *meta*-physics of substance and essence that subsequently dominated Western philosophical thinking, and Heidegger proceeds in the lecture course to discuss the development of this core concern of "metaphysics" in the work of later thinkers. Our focus, though, is on his striking remarks on *physis*, and particularly on his effort to inquire afresh into that equiprimordial "second meaning" of the ancient word *physis* – "the *prevailing* of what prevails" – which we recognize as his fundamental question (*Grundfrage*) into the matter of Being itself (*Sein selbst*), that is, the Being of beings (in their beingness).

One additional note is needed in advance of a discussion of IM. Already in 1929–30, he sketched out the position, so central in IM, that the ancient Greek words *physis* and *aletheia* must be thought "together" as naming the same fundamental matter:

Yet this word for truth [*aletheia*] in antiquity is as old as philosophy itself. It does not need to be and cannot be more ancient, nor indeed more recent, because the understanding of truth that is spoken out in this primal philosophical word first emerges with philosophizing. The seemingly late emergence of the word is no objection to its fundamental meaning, but the reverse: *its innermost belonging together with the fundamental experience of physis as such.* (30:45, my italics)

To this, Heidegger immediately adds: "Let us keep in mind this primal meaning of truth (the revealedness of prevailing beings, *physis*), and let us now ..." The first part of this sentence might be easily overlooked, but it must not because it is crucial and highly instructive. He is elucidating *aletheia* ("this primal meaning of truth") in terms of *physis* ("the revealedness of prevailing beings"). In other words, *aletheia: physis:* the same. This very point he will bring to full development in IM.

II. The Beginning of Western Philosophy: Interpretation of Anaximander and Parmenides (1932)

The text of this lecture course from the summer semester of 1932, only recently published in the *Gesamtausgabe* (2012), offers a preview of Heidegger's later, better-known elucidations of Anaximander and Parmenides. His reading of Parmenides's poem anticipates his more extensive reading just a few years later in the IM lecture course (1935). After IM, he returned to both these ancient thinkers, and to Heraclitus, in his series of remarkable lecture courses in the early 1940s (GA 54, 55, and 78); and of course, he never ceased to return to them in his later work.

Our focus is on *physis*, and this brings us to a few passages in the early part of his elucidation of Anaximander's fragment. Heidegger inquires into how *chronos*, "time," is employed in the fragment, and to do so he turns to a line from Sophocles's play *Ajax*. In lines 646–7, Ajax says, *"hapanth' ho makros kanarithmetos chronos phuei t' adela kai phanenta kryptetai"* (18) (Long immeasurable time brings all things to light from darkness and then covers them after they have been revealed).[8] Sophocles's words *"chronos phuei"* in this line are especially important to Heidegger, but he begins by observing that the whole line shows that "mighty, immeasurable time" lets everything both appear and disappear (19). "Time has everything in its power," he comments, and thus "time stands in the strictest relation with everything that appears." Yet we must hold in view that "disappearing" also belongs to *appearing* – if we are able to understand "appearing" in the proper and fullest sense. Consequently, "appearing [*Erscheinen*] in this entirely broad sense" is what belongs to "beings as beings." For both Sophocles and Anaximander, according to Heidegger, "appearing" in this broadest and richest sense characterizes the Being of beings, "their Being" – and it is "*this* Being of beings with which time stands in relation" (19). Time thus "brings to appearing" all that is manifest and all that returns to darkness, and for this reason, because of this "knowing," Sophocles spoke of the intimate relation between *chronos* and *phuei*. Heidegger therefore rewrites the sequence of words in Sophocles's line as "*chronos – phuei*" in order to highlight and emphasize the innermost connection between the two words, and he adds, "*Phuein* means to let grow – *physis* [means] growth – what is natural and growing – 'nature'" (19).

In this manner, then, he brings the originary understanding of Being into relation with time – and with *physis*. Although his description of *physis* is not as elaborate as in FCM, he nonetheless takes a step further in this lecture course by seeking to show that *Zeit – Sein – Physis* were thought together by the ancient Greek thinkers. In the section "Being and Time as *Physis*," he restates the caveat that he had made in the earlier lecture course that by *physis* the Greeks were not speaking about "nature" in the narrow sense employed by today's "researchers into nature" (19). Rather, for the Greeks, "nature" names "the warp and woof [*Weben und Walten*] of beings – their Being," and their Being "is *physis – phuein*." The Being of beings – *physis* – is characterized by "appearing," but, again, only in the fullest sense of what appears and what disappears. Only by keeping this in view, he insists, can we understand and appreciate what the Greeks said about *physis* and *phuein*: "Growing, arising from – precisely from the Earth and thereby *emerging*, unfolding itself, laying out openly, showing itself – appearing" (20).

III.   *Introduction to Metaphysics* (1935)

Heidegger's early saying of Being as *physis* (as *aletheia*) culminates in his lecture course at the University of Freiburg during the summer semester of 1935. The text of this lecture course was not published until 1953, and as Fried and Polt have pointed out, it is apparent that Heidegger himself held this statement on Being in the highest regard.[9] In my view, IM is his masterwork of the 1930s, and it is unfortunate that the major themes of this text have been comparatively neglected in the recent Heidegger scholarship as a consequence of the fascination with *Beiträge*.

In any case, I think it is time that we return IM – and the *Seinsfrage* – to the forefront of study and commentary. IM is arguably the clearest and most compelling statement on Being that Heidegger ever composed; nevertheless, our focus here is limited to the matter of Being as *physis* (as *aletheia*). He raises the issue of the Greek understanding of *physis* early on in the lecture course and asks, "Now what does the word *physis* say?" His answer is fully in keeping with what he had said in FCM and BWP:

> [*Physis*] says what emerges from itself (for example, the emergence, the blossoming, of a rose), the unfolding that opens itself up, the coming-into-appearance – in short, the emerging-abiding-prevailing [*das aufgehend-verweilende Walten*]. (15:16)

To this he adds that "*physis* as emergence can be experienced everywhere: for example, in celestial processes (the rising of the sun), in the surging of the sea, in the growth of plants, in the coming forth of animals and human beings from the womb." Yet we recall that in FCM, he had carefully distinguished the "first meaning" of *physis* – that which prevails (beings) – from the "second meaning" – prevailing as such (Being as such). In IM, he makes the same point in a less explicit way:

> But *physis*, the emerging prevailing [itself], is not equivalent to these processes [beings], which we still today count as part of "nature."

This emerging and standing-out-in-itself from itself may not be taken
as just one process among others that we observe in beings. (15:16)

His eye is trained on "the emerging prevailing" (*das aufgehende
Walten*) as such, just as it was in FCM. *Physis* names not only
what prevails (beings in their individual and collective shining-
forth) but also the *prevailing itself* of all that prevails. What he
states more clearly and more decisively in IM, though, is that
physis, as the prevailing of what prevails, *is* Being itself:

> *Die physis ist das Sein selbst, kraft dessen das Seiende erst beobachtbar
> wird und bleibt.*

> *Physis* is Being itself, by virtue of which beings first become and
> remain observable. (15:17)

This one sentence, too often passed over without pause, represents the early Heidegger's culminating and defining statement
on the relation between *physis* and Being itself. There is no quali-
fication and no ambiguity: *Physis is Being itself*. And as I have
shown in the earlier chapters, this is a fundamental position that
Heidegger maintained, in one way or another, for the remainder
of his lifetime of thinking.

Everything – including the gods – emerges from out of *physis*.
As he expresses this here: "Thus *physis* originarily means both
heaven and earth, both the stone and the plant, both the animal
and the human, and human history as the work of humans and
gods; and finally and first of all, it means the gods who themselves stand under this destiny" (16:17). Furthermore, *physis* is
the "emerging, abiding prevailing" that "includes both 'becoming' as well as 'being[ness]' in the narrower sense of fixed con-
tinuity." In other words, *physis* unfolds beings in such a way
that both the movement (becoming) of beings and the abiding
(being-ness) of beings can now be seen as but two aspects of the
single temporal-spatial way or process that is Being itself/*physis*.
Thus the age-old metaphysical distinction between becoming
(potency) and being (act; actuality) is grounded by Heidegger in
the onefold of Being itself/*physis*.

Several other times in the course of IM he makes mention of *physis*, but the most crucial remarks come in §38 and §39. In these passages, his early thinking on *Being–physis–aletheia* is brought into sharpest focus and fullest expression. He begins by observing once more that "we know that Being opens itself to the Greeks as *physis*" (106:108). "The roots *phu-* and *pha-*," he continues, "name the same thing. *Phuein*, the emerging that reposes in itself, is *phainesthai*, lighting-up, self-showing, appearing." The poetry of Pindar (*Olympian Ode IX*) provides further evidence, according to Heidegger, that *phua*, the root word of *physis*, means standing-forth as one truly is. He concludes, then, by affirming that "Being means appearing. This does not mean that appearing is something subsequent to Being, something which from time to time meets up with Being. Being essences *as* appearing [*Sein west als Erscheinen*]" (107/108).

We arrive then at another of the most important – and under-appreciated – passages in IM. The header of §39 gives us in advance the core of the matter for thought: "The unique relation in essence between *physis* and *aletheia* – truth as belonging to the essence of Being." After a few introductory remarks, Heidegger comes to the point: "*Sein west als physis* / Being essences as *physis*" (107:109). He proceeds to unfold this position: "The emerging prevailing is an appearing. As such, it makes manifest. This already implies that Being, appearing, is a letting-step forth from concealment. Insofar as a being as such *is*, it places itself into and stands in *unconcealment, aletheia*." Again, what he states here is in perfect harmony with his statements in the two earlier lecture courses we have discussed – but in IM, Heidegger sees with the utmost clarity the connection in essence of *Being–physis–aletheia*. Thus his early thinking on this central matter culminates with these remarkable lines (which I have numbered for further discussion):

[1] For the Greek essence of truth is possible only as one with the Greek essence of Being as *physis*. [2] On the ground of the unique relation in essence between *physis* and *aletheia*, the Greeks can say: beings as beings are true. [3] The true as such is being [*seiend*]. [4] This says: what shows itself in its prevailing stands

in the unconcealed. [5] The unconcealed as such comes to a stand in showing itself. [6] Truth, as un-concealment, is not an addition to Being. [7] *Truth belongs to the essence of Being.* (107/109–10, his italics)

Let us consider each sentence in turn. [1] "For the Greek essence of truth is possible only as one [*in eins*] with the Greek essence of Being as *physis.*" Fried and Polt's translation of IM is careful and elegant, but they do not capture the full significance of this line. The phrase "*in eins*" is not simply "together with," as they have it, but "*as one*" or "*in oneness.*" Heidegger is making a stronger claim than their translation conveys; that is, he is maintaining that the Greek essence of truth is *one* with the Greek essence of Being as *physis.* [2] "On the ground of the unique relation in essence [*einzigartigen Wesenszusammenhangs*] between *physis* and *aletheia*, the Greeks can say: beings as beings are true." Here, too, previous translations have blunted the significance of Heidegger's words. Manheim translates the key word "*Wesenszusammenhang*" as "essential relationship," and Fried and Polt, in similar fashion, offer "essential relation." These translations do not quite convey Heidegger's subtle emphasis on *Wesen.* The word says that there is a unique relation *in essence* between *physis* and *aletheia.* His emphasis is not that there is an important *relation* between the two, but rather that *physis* and *aletheia* are related *in essence* – indeed, they are "one" and the "same" in essence – and "uniquely" so. By understanding this, then and only then, according to his line of thinking, may we understand how the Greeks could say that "beings as beings are true." In other words, the "appearing," the self-manifestation, of beings that defines the essencing of *physis also* defines the essencing of *aletheia.* "Appearing" or "prevailing itself" is the "truth" of beings.

[3] "The true as such is being [*seiend*]." He reinforces the point of the previous sentence by stating more explicitly that "the true as such" is "being." What he appears to be insisting upon (as I have discussed at length in chapter 1) is that "the true" is *first of all* in "being" and not in the intellect (thought, judgment).[10] This pointedly contravenes Thomas Aquinas's

position on Aristotle's understanding of the proper locus of truth. [4] "This says: what shows itself in its prevailing stands in the unconcealed." This line restates the oneness in essence of *physis* ("what shows itself in its prevailing") and *aletheia* ("the unconcealed"). [5] "The unconcealed as such comes to a stand in showing itself." This is the same point as the previous sentence only with the terms reversed. [6] "Truth, as un-concealment, is not an addition to Being." As with sentence [3], the full significance of this line can be appreciated only in view of the traditional philosophical understanding of "truth" as an "addition" to Being supplied by thought, or more specifically, by the "judgment." Hence, he is countering this traditional position by maintaining that truth (*aletheia*) is not, in the first place, an intellective "addition" to Being; rather, truth is the "same" as Being. That is, *aletheia* is convertible with Being insofar as both *aletheia* and Being name unconcealment, manifestness, in all its dimensions. (7) And this is brought home decisively by Heidegger in his concluding italicized sentence:

Truth belongs to the essence [essencing] *of Being.*

The originality and radicality of Heidegger's fundamental position that Being "is" *physis* "is" *aletheia* is what I have been emphasizing for some time, yet this position is apparently still sufficiently alien to philosophical thinking that even among some contemporary Heidegger scholars, the effort persists to return the principal locus of "truth" to the domain of the human being (Dasein). Yet Heidegger's own words say otherwise – and decisively so. From the late 1920s onward, he became ever more clear and insistent that the primary locus of "truth" is Being as *physis*. The *aletheic character of Being as physis* is Heidegger's distinctive philosophical claim, and IM is one of his most important statements on the matter. A few years after IM, in his 1939 essay on Aristotle's *Physics* B 1, he restated this position that "truth as self-revealing belongs to Being itself: *physis* is *aletheia*."[11] In addition, in the 1943 summer semester lecture course on Heraclitus (GA 55), the "middle" Heidegger unfolded this same theme once again with somewhat different highlights, and I will take a closer look at this lecture course in the next chapter. In any case, the crucial point is that his saying – early, middle, and late – of the core matter is clear; the task for us remains to take to heart what he has said.

Concluding Thought

Being as *physis* as *aletheia*. The unfolding – the "truthing" – of all beings and things. From a perch in Charlestown, Massachusetts, overlooking Boston harbour on a rainy late afternoon in early October, one sees the dark water and the stormy sky above. In the small marina sit quietly white and cream-coloured boats, some with blue-tarped tops. Many have names; one is "Tidings of Joy." Occasionally, a boat with a few people on board motors its way out into the harbour, or one returns. Farther from the marina, in the open of the harbour, a tanker cuts its way through the water accompanied by scurrying tugs. On the far shore, buildings and houses, towers and steeples, are crowded together, and above them planes rise diagonally into the sky. Over to the left, an old bridge, a web of steel painted a rustic green, delivers cars to and fro; white lights beaming in one direction, red lights flickering in the other. One, two, three soggy flags wave in the wind, and gulls, catching the same wind, swoop here and there, their wings stretched out against the low-hanging clouds.

Below is the splintered wooden pier guarded at the far end by stout black posts draped with garlands of heavy iron chain. Rough-hewn stone blocks piled one on top of the other bear the weight of the marina house, and scattered mounds of small blackened rocks appear along the shoreline at low tide. Stubby unkempt bushes, a line of trees, and several rows of autumn's flowers make the transition from water to land, to a gravel path that ropes around the water's edge, and to a small yellow-lined parking lot filled with cars of different colours. Along the path, there are a few walkers and joggers and bike riders. The little parking lot opens to a street busy with people, cars, buses, and rolling trolleys moving about, and a row of low red-brick buildings stand elegantly along the length of the street. Behind and above these buildings are shingled houses and more red-brick buildings, and behind them more still, until the hill reaches the summit.

All is present – city and nature gathered together. The fourfold gathered. Everything unfolded – everything unfolding. A homecoming of all beings and things.

Glimpsed here is what Heidegger glimpsed from the very beginning of his lifetime of thinking: the emerging of all beings and things in the ensemble; their holding and lingering and whiling in appearance, carried along by a great giving stream, a stream not hidden exactly, but difficult to see. This great giving flow, this temporal-spatial letting of all things, is Being – but also *physis*, *aletheia*. Indeed, in our relation to *physis* it is no doubt important to keep in view that it is we mortals who bring into language what emerges and lingers and passes away. There is no overlooking ourselves as "the shepherd" and "the guardian" of Being/*physis*. Yet in Heidegger's distinctive vision and version of "phenomenology," we are always called to recall that ours is an *Entsprechung*, a cor-respondence. *Physis* first addresses us, and ever so. *Physis* calls forth from us language and saying and meaning. *Physis* opens us so that we may open up a world of meaning. The core matter for Heidegger – and for those inclined to his thinking – is that *physis* is the measure, not Dasein. Nevertheless, this by no means diminishes the human being, not at all. It is simply to recognize the *limit* of our marvellous *logos*, our comprehensibility (*Verstehbarkeit*), our taking-as, our meaning-making. Manifestation structurally precedes and exceeds any kind and any level of meaning. There is a depth to manifestation that is never exhausted by sense or meaning – in Heidegger's own words,

this truth of Being does not exhaust itself in Dasein.[12]

This is the reserve he so often spoke of as the *lethe* of *aletheia* or the *kryptesthai* of Heraclitus's saying *physis kryptesthai philei,* "nature loves to hide." It is the dimension of "earth" in relation to "world" – the "sheltering" (*bergen*) that is intrinsic to *physis*.

We take in all that we are able – yet we realize there is more, always more, to manifestation – a richness of showing, a reserve of appearing, that can never be fully tapped. *Physis* endlessly arising and we endlessly astonished.

Chapter 5

Sentinels of Being

[The] *physis* itself is the self-showing that essentially shows itself in the signs.

Heidegger, from the lecture course

Kosmos [as *physis*] shimmers ungraspably throughout all things.

Heidegger, Seminar in Le Thor, 1969

Where the Biscayne Bay opens to the mouth of the Miami River in Miami, Florida, a small outcropping of land was once part of the ancient home of the Native American people, the Tequesta. In the last century, that modest showing of land was transformed by human efforts into a sizeable, nearly perfect triangular landform called the Brickell Key, which is now the home of expensive condominiums and their residents. Yet these people of a later day and their fancy built forms still share the place with nature's effusion. Royal purple and fuchsia blossoms of the bougainvillea are clustered along the walking paths; date and coconut palms sway gently in the breezes, their fronds whispering to one another; small birds dart back and forth all the while chirping and chattering away; and ancient-looking iguanas sun themselves imperturbably in a jumble of scraggly bushes at the water's edge.

At one corner of the Brickell Key, named Tequesta Point, rises a bronze sculpture by the Cuban-born sculptor Manuel Carbonell.[1] Raised high on a trapezoidal base of coral stone, a thick, muscular, immensely powerful man of the Tequesta people holds up to his mouth with both hands a magnificent conch shell and blows into it joyously. The sculpture bears the name *El Centinela del Rio*, "The Sentinel of the River." Despite the massiveness of the sculpted body, a vital energy flows freely through it. The right leg is thrust forward while the left leg pushes off the ground, with the left foot planted almost perpendicularly to the right leg and foot. The effect is to give the figure a decisive forward momentum. The sentinel is not just blowing mightily into the great conch shell, he is almost leaping ahead to do so. There is for this Tequesta man anticipation, passion, celebration, sheer joy, unending joy, in sounding the spiral shell instrument again and again.

The sculpted figure is a "sentinel." This word might too easily call to mind a military or prison "guard" of some kind, but this "sentinel" has little to do with these sorts of tasks. We must consider more thoughtfully what the word "sentinel" means; that is, we must consider what this word fundamentally conveys. The word in both English and Spanish is derived from the Latin *sentire*, to feel, to perceive, or more broadly to receive and take in. A "sentinel," then, in its root meaning, is one who is open to and receives and takes in what is; one who "senses" all that is. The "sentinel," in other words, is one who is fully alive and alert and awake to all that comes and arrives, and in this manner is the one who "guards" – better, "safeguards" – all that approaches and shows itself. Yet the "sentinel" is not only alert to everything that approaches but also *alerts* others to what approaches. Carbonell's "sentinel" responds to the approach of everything by joyously sounding the conch shell so that others, too, may become fully alert and awake to the approach of the manifest. In this way, the "sentinel" is also a "herald" of what comes and arrives, announcing and proclaiming in word or song or sound all that comes-to-pass.

The "sentinel" as "herald" makes manifest what is manifest. Certainly, there is a peculiar joy in any such making-manifest, in making the conch shell sing with delight; but the greater joy, the more fundamental and profound joy, that overcomes Carbonell's "sentinel" as "herald" is the joy of the approach of the manifest, of all that arrives in its arriving. The song of the conch shell announces the presence of the pastel green waters of the river and the bay, the soft blue of the sky above and the softer white clouds passing by, and the soaring gulls and the ragged pelicans who patrol the waters. But, too, there is present the busy port across the bay with its behemoth cruise ships and tankers and container ships; the giant hoisting cranes bent at the water's edge much like the elegant long-necked birds at a watering hole; and the multitude of buildings, houses, and festive tents rising from the grounds nearby. And people everywhere: on the ships, around the ships, on small boats and skiffs in the bay, in shopping pavilions, and on all the paths that wind around the sea walls, people walking, running, bicycling, sitting, talking, daydreaming. The night arrives as well, and the "sentinel" heralds its arrival and the exhilarating array of city lights and the shimmering moonlight on the dark, mysterious waters. The "sentinel" is there, always there, day and night, sounding the conch shell to celebrate the presence of everything, all beings and things, the sacred and the profane, the high and the low, the deep and the shallow. All is joyfully heralded simply because it "is."

~⸙~

Being ever approaches and "hails" Dasein, Heidegger tells us, so Carbonell's sculpture puts us in touch with the core of Heidegger's thinking, with the essential concern of what we might still refer to, if properly understood, as his *hermeneutic* phenomenology. That is, the *"hermeneut"* is the Hermes-like messenger of what is, the one who is open to Being's approach and who announces, heralds, proclaims to all others the temporal-spatial presencing of all beings and things. Like Carbonell's "sentinel," Heidegger's *hermeneut* is enraptured by Being – the One way that manifests All, the *hen-panta, physis,* Nature – and is moved to make a joyful noise. The *hermeneut* cor-responds to Being – and it is Being that is celebrated. The *hermeneut* is, in the first place, pointing to Being and not simply to the "pointing." How odd, then, that so many contemporary Heidegger commentators have come to focus on the "pointing," that is, the "meaning-making" of the human being, as the core concern of Heidegger's thinking. It is as if they hear the sound of the great conch shell and focus *only* on the sound! Unfortunately, this emphasis on Dasein's meaning-making, taken in even the broadest sense, perpetuates the very "forgottenness" of Being that Heidegger so often lamented, and it represents a falling back into the "subjectivism" of the modern philosophy of consciousness and language that he strove so tirelessly to overcome. In response, then, let us once again recall what has been forgotten: the presencing, the emerging, of all that is, Being–*physis–aletheia*–the primordial *Logos*.

In previous chapters, I have commented on a number of different texts to make this point in several different ways, but here I would like to take up this core matter of Heidegger's thinking by highlighting and discussing several important passages from his two lecture courses on Heraclitus, which he delivered in consecutive summer semesters in 1943 and 1944 at the University of Freiburg. This chapter focuses on the 1943 lecture course; the following chapter will address the one from 1944. Both lecture courses are collected in Volume 55 of the *Gesamtausgabe*, which has not been translated into English even though it was first published in the German in 1979.[2] These elucidations are among Heidegger's most brilliant and seminal, but they are also exceedingly congested with involved arguments and intricate wordplay, which no doubt has put off any number of would-be translators. Still, in time this volume will be become available in English translation, and it will serve the scholarship well – besides confirming yet again just how decisive Heidegger's turn to Being had become by the early 1940s.

The editor of Volume 55 (as well as Volume 54: *Parmenides*) was Manfred Frings, whom I came to know in the late 1980s. He was a founding member of the Heidegger Circle in the United States in the 1960s and an exceptionally careful and thoughtful reader of Heidegger's work. Moreover, he was a lovely man, wonderfully engaged and engaging, kind and generous with his time and knowledge, and a true lover of the rugged beauty of the American West and Southwest. Manfred had a special interest in these commentaries on the early Greek thinkers, and he considered it a high honour that Heidegger had entrusted to him the task of editing these volumes. Some years later (in 1990 and 1991) he published two articles, one on each of the lecture courses on Heraclitus, which are careful overviews in English of Heidegger's slow and difficult thinking on Heraclitus's sayings.[3] Not long before his death in 2008, I corresponded with him once again, and among other things, he recalled and impressed upon me Heidegger's lifelong desire to find new ways, always another way, of bringing Being itself into view. In his perspective, Heidegger never rested content with any one of his formulations of the core matter for thought that he always kept before him.

Frings's articles on the two lecture courses on Heraclitus provide a good basic summary of Heidegger's readings such that we need not go over the same ground in the same way. Yet there remain key passages and points that were not highlighted by Frings and that have become more relevant and significant given the current concerns in the Heidegger scholarship, and to these I would particularly like to turn.

I.   The 1943 Lecture Course on Heraclitus: "The Inception of Western Thinking"

A.   Physis *and Manifestation: "The Ever-Living Fire"*

To orient ourselves, this lecture course is fundamentally an excursus on the ancient Greek understanding of *physis* as Heidegger saw the matter in the early 1940s – the "middle" Heidegger, so to speak. As I noted in the previous chapters, the theme of Being as *physis* was a central and lifelong concern for Heidegger, and much of what he had to say about *physis* both before and after this particular lecture course is clearly in evidence here. Yet there is a richness (and complexity) to his elucidations in this text that is distinctive of this period. After several opening remarks on Heraclitus, the man and the thinker, Heidegger moves on to argue for a new ordering of the fragments, and he wishes to place fragment 16 in the first position because it is the determinative "centre" of so many of the fragments:

to me dunon pote pos an tis lathoi;

Heidegger's translation: *"Dem ja nicht Untergehen(den) je, wie möchte irgendwer (dem) verborgen sein?"* (44)

English translation of Heidegger's translation: "From not ever setting, how could anyone be concealed?"

In a series of detailed observations and word explications (44–101), he makes the case that the "not-ever-setting" (*to me dunon pote*) spoken of in the fragment means the same as the "ever-emerging" (*immerdar Aufgehen*), which for the earliest Greek thinkers characterized their experience of *physis*. Yet *physis*, he points out, was but another name for Being (*einai* and the word *on* in its participial form and verbal sense) as it was originarily experienced by the Greeks, and he proceeds in a familiar fashion to discuss how the originary experience of Being as *physis* was later progressively transformed into the metaphysical foundational notion of the being(ness) of beings. The earliest Greek experience and thinking of Being as *physis* was thereby closed off and "forgotten" from the beginning of the metaphysical tradition of thinking, and a *"Seinsvergessenheit"* continues unabated to the present day (83). Nevertheless, the Greeks experienced *physis* (as Being itself) as "the pure emerging" (*das reine Aufgehen*), and for them, all beings and things – "mountain and sea, plant and animal, houses and human beings, gods and the heavens" – emerged from out of this pure emerging (102–3). Furthermore, the Greeks also named this experience of "pure emerging" as *"zoe."* (94). According to Heidegger, the Greeks experienced *everything* as "living" (*zoe*) insofar as everything emerges from out of the pure emerging itself. And since this pure emerging (unconcealing) was also experienced and named by the Greeks as *aletheia*, the Greek *Ur*-words *physis, zoe, aletheia* all say "the same" and illuminate, each in a somewhat different manner, Being itself (96, 103).

After this lengthy discussion through which he establishes his basic reading of the pivotal fragment 16, Heidegger proceeds to a reading of the other sayings in the light of 16. One of the most important is fragment 123, which he took up many times over the course of his lifetime, each time with a slightly different rendering and reading. Here he translates the fragment this way:

physis kryptesthai philei

Heidegger's translation: "*Das Aufgehen dem Sichverbergen schenkt's die Gunst.*" (110)

English translation of Heidegger's translation: "Emerging bestows favour upon self-concealing."

While all students of Heidegger's work are familiar with the importance and significance of this Heraclitean fragment for his thinking, many may not realize that one of his most elaborate elucidations of the fragment is to be found in this lecture course. The details of his commentary are interesting in their own right, but for our purposes, we may highlight that his fundamental approach to the fragment is essentially the same as for all of his other readings over the years: Being as *physis* is the temporal arising-setting (showing-withholding) of all beings and things. *Physis* itself is this arising-setting and therefore is not any particular "being." For this reason, *physis* is (comparatively) "inapparent" (*unscheinbar*). *Physis* "prevails throughout" (*durchwalten*) all beings and things and is therefore "manifest" precisely as this "prevailing" and not as a particular being or thing. Heidegger, as he reads Heraclitus's other sayings, calls this peculiar and proper "manifestation" (*Offenbarkeit*) of *physis* the inapparent "harmony" (*harmonia*), the resplendent "cosmos" (*kosmos*), and the ever-emerging and ever-living "fire" (*pur*), as well as the "lightning flash" that "steers" all things (160–71; fragments 64, 66, 30, 124). That Being itself is "manifest" in its own proper way is an important feature of Heidegger's thinking that is often overlooked by commentators. Being as *physis* is "inapparent" – but *only* in the sense that it does not appear as *a being*. Yet Being is most certainly "manifest" to those who can truly "see," such as the earliest Greek thinkers. As he puts the matter succinctly in the lecture course, "*Physis* is the inapparent shining" (144). In fact, as I discussed in chapter 2, this distinctive manifestness of Being is what, later in his life, he elaborated in a beautifully poetic way as "the gleaming of Nature" in his commentary on one of Hölderlin's "last poems."

B.   Physis *and* Aletheia *and Being*

We may forgo other details of Heidegger's readings in order to address several important passages at the end of the lecture course that Frings, given his concerns at the time, did not discuss at length. In chapter 4, I highlighted how the early Heidegger understood *physis* and *aletheia* as "one" in essence. He makes the same case in this lecture course, in a passing fashion early on (as I noted above), but in a more deliberate and decisive manner in the concluding sections. In §8b (171–4), he states that fragment 30 shows that both the gods and human beings must be understood as shining-forth from out of *physis* – indeed, that no one and nothing "can be concealed before *physis*" (172). And he adds:

> The fragment inquires into the relation of *physis*, that is, the *kosmos* as the originary resplendence, to the gods and human beings. The emerging resplendence is "beyond" them because gods and human beings, insofar as they are, only are as they emerge into the open and in this way can never be concealed before the open. (173)

The "essence" of *physis* is this "resplendent" (but "inapparent") temporal emerging-withholding of all things, including the gods and human beings. Yet this hidden "harmony" of rising-setting is the same as "unconcealment" (*Unverborgenheit*), which the Greeks named *aletheia* and which we have come to call "truth" (*Wahrheit*). What this means, he concludes, is that "we now recognize that in [our] first attempt to think the first fragment [that is, the pivotal fragment 16], *aletheia* is thought in it, though it is not named" (173). Consequently, understood in their "essencing," *physis* and *aletheia* say the same. The earliest Greek thinkers had a glancing understanding of this, but they could not thematize it as such. That is for us the task for thinking.

He then briefly returns to fragment 16 in order to read it explicitly in terms of *aletheia*. The "never-setting" that is the "ever-emerging" that is *physis* is also *aletheia*, provided that we always keep in view that *aletheia* is un-concealment, that is, emergence from out of concealment. We must always consider fragment 16 in relation to fragment 123: "Emergence bestows favour upon self-concealing." *Physis* and *aletheia* are the same in this way. Yet having made this clear, he has one more important point to make regarding *aletheia*: *aletheia* must, in the first place, be understood as the way that Being "is" and not as any kind of function or activity of human knowing or cognition. First and foremost, *aletheia* ("truth" understood in an originary and primordial manner) refers to the peculiar and proper manifestness of Being and not to the manifestive activity of the human being as this has been maintained in one way or another in the long tradition of philosophical thinking in the West:

> The thinking of metaphysics knows truth only as a feature of cognition. That is why the hint presently given – that "truth," in the sense of *aletheia*, is the inception of the essence of *physis* itself and of the gods and humans belonging therein – remains strange in every respect for all previous thinking. Yes, it is even good and crucial that we hold fast to this strange matter and not be persuaded hastily that *aletheia* is not, as metaphysics up until now has meant in a "self-evident" manner, a mere feature of cognitive comportment – but rather is the fundamental feature of Being itself [*der Grundzug des Seins selbst*]. (175)

Physis "is" *aletheia* "is" Being itself. This is Heidegger's original and distinctive position, as I have maintained all along, but he states the case with particular clarity and emphasis in this passage. He leaves no room for doubt: *aletheia*, in the first place, "is the fundamental feature of Being itself" and not of the human being. Indeed, we must learn from the ancient Greeks how to comport ourselves once again to *Being as aletheia*, to attend to "the truth of Being" rather than only to the "truth" as defined and determined by our own "sense-making" capability and activity.

C. Physis *Itself Is the Self-Showing and Giving of Signs*

That Heidegger's focal point in 1943 is the manifestation of Being is further underscored by his concluding reflection in the lecture course. Admittedly, his remarks in this final section are difficult and cryptic, but since the point he attempts to make is especially important for our purposes, it is worth our effort to follow his reading closely. He begins by recalling that at the beginning of the lecture course he had observed that the goddess Artemis and her distinctive "signs" (*Zeichen*) of the "bow and lyre" were centrally important to Heraclitus. Her signs, he states, have helped bring into view the peculiar essence of *physis* as the hidden "joining" (*Fügung*) of the rising-setting, bringing apart-bringing together, of all beings and things. To this he adds: "Bearing the same sign is Apollo, the brother of the goddess Artemis. He is, along with his sister Artemis, *the* god of Heraclitus" (177). Heidegger cites fragment 93 as naming Apollo and observes that "Heraclitus says here in which way Apollo is the one looking-in and appearing and how in his appearing he gives a hint unto Being. The god himself must, in the manner that he is the god, correspond to Being, that is, to the essence of *physis*" (177). Thus the fragment:

ho anax hou to manteion esti to en Delphois oute legei oute kruptei alla semainei

Heidegger's translation: "*Der Hohe, dessen Ort der weisenden Sage der in Delphi ist, weder entbirgt er (nur), noch verbirgt er (nur), sondern er gibt Zeichen.*" (177)

English translation of Heidegger's translation: "The high one, whose place of the pointing-saying is in Delphi, neither uncovers (only) nor conceals (only); rather he gives signs."

According to Heidegger, "*legein* is here [in the fragment] clearly used [by Heraclitus] as the counter-word to *kryptein* and means, therefore, [what is] in opposition to 'concealing,' 'uncovering.'" He finds in this particular reference to *legein* a confirmation of his own reading of *legein* as "*lesen*" in terms of "gathering" (*sammeln/Sammlung*). His comments here are rudimentary and not fully worked out, but we recognize in these brief remarks a preview of the lecture course on Heraclitus that he would offer the very following summer in 1944, which concerned the earliest Greek thinking on the primordial *Logos* and on the *homologein* of the human being. (I take up this lecture course in the following chapter.) What he wishes to emphasize in the text we are presently considering is that "gathering" is closer to the originary meaning of the ancient Greek word *legein* than other later philosophical terms such as "reasoning." Although in the 1944 lecture course he will distinguish carefully between the human being's "gathering" (*legein/homologein*) and the fundamental and primordial "fore-gathering" (*Versammlung*) of Being as the primordial *Logos*, here the matter is not so clearly articulated. Consequently, he appears to use *legein* with respect both to how Being fundamentally "is" and to how the human being fundamentally cor-responds to Being. Accordingly, he states rather obliquely that "*logos* – another fundamental word of Heraclitus' – means for Heraclitus neither a 'teaching' [*Lehre*] nor 'discourse' [*Rede*] nor 'meaning' [*Sinn*], but rather the uncovering 'gathering' – in the sense of the primordially joining One of the inapparent joining." The next two sentences are more direct and instructive:

> [The names] *logos – harmonia – physis – kosmos* say the Same [*das Selbe*], but each time as a different originary determination of Being. We learn here in the first place to get a sense of which way the earliest thinkers were able to glimpse and say the richness of the Simple. (178)

Even so, the matter is not so simple because the Simple (Being) unfolds as *legein* (uncovering, gathering) and *kryptein* (concealing). Therefore, the primordial "letting-appear" and "making-manifest,"

which he states is his core concern, he names, following the words
of the fragment, *semainein*; that is, Apollo "gives a sign" (*ein Zeichen
geben*). This final step is most puzzling. It is not at all immediately
clear how *semainein* – Apollo's "giving signs" – is a proper characterization of Being as *physis* as the temporal revealing-concealing
unfolding-way wherein and whereby all beings and things issue
forth. Clearly, more needs to be said, and he proceeds to explicate
this unusual conclusion.

He starts off by dismissing all previous readings of this fragment as "thoughtlessly nonsensical" and observes that the god
Apollo must be understood to be giving an indication about
what is essential (*das Wesenhafte*). But what is essential is *physis*, the "emerging and self-concealing" (179). If the god were
only to uncover or only to conceal, he tells us, then the god
would utterly fail to correspond to the essence of *physis*. Apollo,
however, does not simply uncover or simply conceal, but rather
draws together uncovering and concealing into a more primordial Oneness (*Einheit*). "But this happens," he states, "insofar
as he [Apollo] gives signs" (179). "Then what is a sign?" Heidegger asks rhetorically.

The question is answered in several involved sentences, and
his language is certainly an obstacle to a clear understanding
of what he is getting at. Nonetheless, his basic point is that the
sign is "something that is shown, therefore uncovered" but at
the same time indicative of what is not-shown, not-appearing.
Therefore, "the essence of the sign is the uncovering-concealing
[*die entbergende Verbergung*]," and "the showing of the sign" [*das
Zeigen des Zeichens*] is precisely this primordial uncovering-
concealing. He concludes by observing that the sign, so understood, thus makes manifest in accordance with the essence of
physis that has been carefully elucidated in the lecture course.
Consequently:

> *Die physis selbst ist das Sichzeigende, das wesenhaft sich in den Zeichen
> zeigt.* (179)

> [The] *physis* itself is the self-showing that essentially shows itself
> in the signs.

This is a striking conclusion, but what does it tell us? What exactly is the matter that Heidegger is so concerned to convey in this final reflection of the lecture course? It must be admitted that this is difficult to say. Nevertheless, I think that despite the challenges posed by his rhetoric, we can discern the fundamental matter that is moving and compelling his thinking, namely, that *physis* itself (Being itself) is the point of the pointing of the sign. But let us approach this matter more deliberately.

In his distinctive way, what Heidegger appears to be vigorously arguing against is all philosophical conceptions of the "sign" (language) as merely a subjective, mental phenomenon. His insistence is that the "sign," in Greek *sema, semeion, semainein*, must be thought, along with the earliest Greek thinkers, as "giving" Being itself (as *physis* as *aletheia*). Thus he notes in the next paragraph of the text that "signs," thought in a Greek way, are "the self-showing of emerging itself" and "are nothing that is made or contrived." This latter position he finds prevailing in contemporary thinking "and its metaphysics" (179–80). He points specifically to Nietzsche's position that "truth" is no more than a willed "value" as "already at the most extreme distance from the [originary] essence of truth." And precisely this wayward thinking continues to dominate philosophy with its preoccupation with "logic" and mere linguistic and propositional analysis. Heidegger's creative reading of fragment 93, then, is really meant as a stern critique of the modern philosophy of consciousness, inaugurated particularly by Descartes, and its focus on the "*ego cogito*" or "subject" that is self-contained, isolated, and locked away with its "signs" (language) with no possible access to Being. In this modern philosophical perspective – which Heidegger ultimately thought that Husserl, too, shared – language is empty, a mere matter of signs or signifiers that can be analysed and manipulated at will. It is this modern "subjectivism" or "subjecticity" – this peculiarly modern form of the "forgottenness of Being" – that Heidegger was determined to break through once and for all. *Physis* itself (Being itself) shows itself in the "sign."

So far, so good perhaps. Yet we must not miss another crucial aspect of his elucidation of the fragment. His phrasing of the core matter remains surprising; it is Apollo (*physis*) who "gives signs," and the key sentence states that "*physis* itself is the self-showing that essentially shows itself in the signs." All that I have noted above regarding his position remains perfectly sound, I think, but it appears that Heidegger wishes to push the matter even further. It seems that in his effort to decisively overcome the subjectivism of the modern period and to return our attention to Being, he deliberately expresses the core matter in such a way that it is Apollo (*physis* itself, Being itself) that is the "giver" of signs! In other words, he is bold enough to let Heraclitus's words – Heraclitus, the Obscure – speak for his own position here. Indeed, how strange and "obscure" it is to say that Being "gives signs." What could this mean? We all know that only human beings have and use "signs" and "language." It is something of a philosophical scandal to say that Being "gives signs." Precisely. By stating the core issue in this way, Heidegger forces us to look past ourselves and see that it is Being-*physis* that always and everywhere addresses us and compels our cor-respondence. So *remark*-able is this "address" and "appeal" of Being to us that we may say that it is Being – the appearing of all that is – that gives language, that is, compels language or gathers language. Of course, his saying of this may be cryptic, much like Heraclitus's own sayings, and therefore certainly immensely frustrating to the usual reader of philosophical texts, but, on the other hand, this very poetic and enigmatic manner of expression may be said to be the true genius of Heidegger's way of thinking.

Concluding Thought

Near the end of the lecture course, Heidegger observes: "The word, wherein the essence of the historical human being is given over to itself, is the word of Beyng [*Seyn*]" (180). This phrase "the word *of* Beyng" says two things. First, the word (sign, language) is, in the first place, not a mental entity, but rather that which brings into manifestation what manifests itself. It is Being that is present to us in language, not simply our own mental constructions. In fact, this point is of such importance to Heidegger – a point that he did not think was sufficiently made by Husserl's critique of the Cartesian position – that his phrase is also meant to say that the word "belongs" to Being. That is, what comes to us, what arrives to us, is already so pregnant with "word" that we are only the midwife in bringing the word to birth. The self-showing that is Being-*physis* is already "*wordable*," we might say, as it comes to us, and we cor-respond in word (and sound and image and movement). Our cor-respondence hails the hailing. In this way, we are indeed the heralds, the sentinels, of Being.

Chapter 6

"This *Logos* Is Being Itself"

The *Logos* is accordingly something hearable, a kind of speech and voice; but manifestly not the voice of a human being.

Heidegger, from the lecture course

True obedience,
silently the flowers speak
to the inner ear.

Onitsura

Finally, let us turn our attention to Heidegger's lecture course on Heraclitus that he presented the following summer semester in 1944. As I have mentioned, the 1943 and 1944 lecture courses on Heraclitus, as important as they are, have not yet been translated into English, and commentators have not mined their many riches. The German title of the 1944 lecture course, *Logik. Heraklits Lehre vom Logos*, already gives us to consider that Heidegger's focus is on Heraclitus's "teaching" (*Lehre*) as it issues forth *from* the primordial *Logos*.[1] That is, we are called upon to "listen" to Being as the primordial *Logos*. What emerges distinctly in these elucidations is that Heidegger's concern is first and foremost with bringing into view and affirming the primacy of Being as the primordial *Logos* in "relation" (*Bezug, Beziehung*) to the *logos* of the human being.

I. A Note on the Discussion on "Logic"

In a prefatory note to the text, Heidegger states that the basic aim of the lecture course is to arrive at "the primordial logic," and this means to arrive once again at the thinking "of" the primordial *Logos* as was attained by Heraclitus. Even so, he does not begin the lectures by immediately engaging Heraclitus's sayings on the *Logos*; rather, he builds up to this task by way of a lengthy excursus on what "logic" has come to mean in Western thinking. Much of what he has to say in these sections follows the broad lines of his thinking in previous years on the problem of "logic." Since much has already been written on the topic of his critique of logic, I would prefer to move on to important passages regarding his readings of Heraclitus that have received little, if any, scholarly attention. There is, however, one matter addressed by Heidegger in these sections on "logic" that I would like to highlight because it underscores the significance of his later statements on Being as the primordial *Logos*.

He inquires into how "logic is the metaphysics of the *logos*" (253). Logic, as it developed with Plato and Aristotle, is most properly concerned with the statement, *die Aussage*, that asserts something about something, in the Greek, *legein ti kata tinos*. Yet what is stated presupposes that something has already been "addressed" (Heidegger's word is *Ansprechen, angesprochen*) as "what it is." That which is addressed (*das Angesprochene*) means that it is "experienced as appearing," as "showing itself." For Heidegger, what "logic" refers to as the "subject" of a "statement" is traceable back to an experience of its appearing and showing, its shining-forth. This appearance of something he refers to more specifically as the "external appearance" (*das Aussehen*) that something offers. Thus, for instance, "that there which appears, that house there, for example, shows itself in looking at it, and [it] stands in the external appearance of 'house' and 'houseness' and *is* thus *a* house" (253; his italics). Likewise, he observes, there appears "the book" in its "bookness."

The first thing we note is that Heidegger's line of thinking affirms the *ontological* basis of logical statements; that is,
logical terms are rooted in our encounter with what-is. Yet
his concern extends further. He wishes to show that the *Aussehen*, the sheer "external appearance" of things as they show
themselves from themselves, becomes in Plato the "what-
being," the "whatness" of things, which is elevated to the
"being[ness] of beings." Plato is the one who for the "first
time" thought the "being[ness] of beings" in terms of the pure
external appearance of that which shines forth. This external
appearance as such was called by Plato and the other Greek
thinkers the *eidos* and *idea* (in German, *Idee*, and in English,
"idea"). The sheer appearance of something, the "houseness"
of the house or the "bookness" of the book or the "treeness" of
the tree, became for Plato the principal and guiding thought
of his thinking and for all subsequent "metaphysical" thinking. *Meta*-physics from Plato onward became defined by this
preoccupation with the "non-sensuous" or "supra-sensuous"
idea (form, *essentia*, essence) (254).

Thus to bring this back to the matter of "logic." Heidegger
observes that in a statement such as "the house is high," the sub-
ject-word "house" is not contrived or constructed but ultimately
refers back directly to the experience of the house in its "houseness" and is thus relatable back to the *eidos* of the house. In this
sense, then, the *logos* of "logic" is intimately related to the *eidos* of
metaphysics. The *logos* of "logic" proceeds *only* by way of a consideration of the "ideas," and this is most in evidence in all categorial
propositions, for as he notes, "*kategoria* is the statement [in logic] in
the exemplary sense" (255). Therefore, since logic can think only in
metaphysical terms, he concludes that "logic is the metaphysics of
the *logos*." This *logos* of "logic" and "metaphysics" – the *logos* pre-
occupied with the *eidos* – has dominated Western philosophy ever
since Plato. In the modern philosophy of consciousness, however,
there is a twist: a decisive turn towards understanding the *eidos* as
generated or constituted by the human *logos*. Consequently, the
legacy of the modern philosophy of consciousness is to regard the
human *logos* as the "measure" of all that is. Yet how differently
does Heraclitus speak about the *Logos*!

II.   **"This *Logos* Is Being Itself"**

After the lengthy excursus on the origin and development of
"logic," Heidegger turns his attention to the elucidation of a number of Heraclitus's sayings on the *Logos*. It is his convention in
this lecture course to use the capital "L" (that is, the capital of the
Greek letter *lamda*) when referring to what he calls "the primordial
Logos" (*der ursprüngliche Logos*) in distinction from *logos* understood as the *legein* or *homologein* of the human being. As we shall
see, in the concluding paragraphs of the lecture course he will also
use the capital Greek letter in writing *Physis* and *Aletheia* – since
Physis, *Aletheia*, and the primordial *Logos* all say "the same," that
is, Being itself. He begins the "way back" to a consideration of
the "pre-metaphysical" understanding of the *Logos* with a "clarifying" translation of the saying of Heraclitus that is fragment 50:

*ouk emou, alla tou logou akousantas homologein sophon estin hen panta
einai*

Heidegger's translation: *"Habt ihr nicht bloss mich angehört, sondern
habt ihr (ihm gehorsam, horchsam) auf den Logos gehört, dann ist Wissen
(das darin besteht), mit dem Logos das Gleiche sagend zu sagen: Eins ist
alles."* (243)

English translation of Heidegger's translation: "Your having listened not merely to me, but rather to the *Logos* (obediently, heark-
eningly to it), then knowing (which therein consists) is to say
sayingly along with the *Logos* the very same thing: One is All."

A few years later, in 1951, he delivered a lecture to the Bremen
Club, published as "*Logos* (Heraclitus, Fragment B 50)," which
is better-known than his discussion of the fragment in this lecture course.[2] Again, rather than go over ground that has been
covered before, I would prefer to attend to certain key passages
that give us fresh perspectives on his thinking. Nevertheless,
we should take note of two of his most basic points in reading
this particular fragment. First, "*legein*" is to be understood fundamentally as "to glean" and "to gather" (*lesen / sammeln*). To

gather is also to preserve, shelter, spare, protect, and safeguard. Second, Heraclitus's words *hen panta* should be understood as the one *Ur*-phenomenon – *hen-panta* – because this expression tells us how the primordial *Logos* "is," namely, that Being as the primordial *Logos* is the One temporal unfolding way wherein and whereby All beings and things come forth, issue forth, shine forth. "One is All" (*Eins ist alles*).

The primordial *Logos* is a gathering (*Sammlung*) of all that is or, more precisely, a "fore-gathering" (*Versammlung*). In other words, the *Logos* has always already laid out and gathered and safeguarded all beings prior to (*im Vorhinein, zuvor*) any other kind of selective "gathering." Heidegger is especially fond of this word "*Versammlung*" (which he also often writes as *Ver-sammlung*), and he refers to it as a "wonderful word" in the lecture course (268). In everyday German, this word most commonly means an "assembly" of people, but as he uses the word in the elucidation, it is exceedingly difficult to translate into English. Frings's suggestion of "fore-gathering" is a good one (and he is well aware that the prefix *ver* is not *vor*). "Fore-gathering" comes very close to conveying Heidegger's indications; thus, we may render an important line this way: "The *Logos* is the safeguarding fore-gathering that as the One unifies beings as a whole, and thus as the Being of beings as a whole, [the *Logos*] shines throughout and in its light lets shine forth [all beings]" (333).

This sentence illustrates Heidegger's thinking throughout the lecture course concerning the *Seinsfrage*. What he has to say about the "question of Being" is one of the most interesting and instructive aspects of his discussion – and overlooked by commentators. In fact, his remarks show clearly and decisively – once again – that contemporary commentators who claim that his abiding core concern was not with Being itself are missing the mark. So, for example, after bringing into view how "logic" thinks the *logos* metaphysically, he states:

How it stands with metaphysics and its core-essence, that is, with "logic" and with the *logos* thought in this way, is that it is only another form of the question concerning what metaphysics questions insofar as it questions one thing: what is the being [*das Seiende*]? (276)

But he then adds:

> Yet how it stands with Being itself [*Sein selbst*], how it [Being itself]
> essences and prevails in its truth, metaphysics does not and never
> questions, and this [is so] because metaphysics cannot ask this
> question and cannot bring it into question, if metaphysics is to
> remain what it is. (276)

He is perfectly clear that the *Erfragte* – that which we are
seeking in our questioning beyond metaphysical thinking
about beings in their beingness – is Being itself. To think along
with Heraclitus regarding the primordial *Logos* is to bring into
view Being itself. Moreover, a few paragraphs later he adds
that Being itself (here named Beyng itself, *das Seyn selbst*) is
the genuine (*eigentlich*) to-be-thought (*Zu-denkende*) and "that
nothing higher, nothing more primordial, nothing more present, but also nothing more inapparent and nothing more inde-
structible can be thought than Beyng itself" (278). I do not think
that Heidegger could have been more clear, direct, or emphatic
than this.

Furthermore, he clarifies this point in a way that stands in
even starker contrast to the position of those contemporary commentators who argue that it is Dasein and Dasein's constitutive
meaning-making or coping-activity that is the core concern of his
thinking. Heidegger tells us that Being itself as the primordial
Logos, "the pre-metaphysical *Logos*," is not "any kind of activity
of human saying or stating" (277). This is crucial. The essencing
of *Logos* is not reducible to formal statements or assertions or
propositions or any form of meaning; *nor is it reducible to any kind
of human "saying" (Sagen)*. Simply put, the primordial *Logos* is not
reducible to any activity of the human being.

If there is any doubt about this, we need only attend to Heidegger's words as he amplifies his point:

> The *logos* of the customarily so-called logic is, as statement and
> saying, an activity and capability of the human being. This *logos*
> belongs to the being that the human being is. The *Logos* of which
> Heraclitus speaks is the gathered and the gathering as the One

that unifies everything, and not as any feature within a being. This *Logos* is the primordial fore-gathering that preserves the being as the being that it is. *This Logos is Being itself wherein all beings essence* [come-to-presence, unfold]. Reflecting on this *Logos* is certainly not more logic in the usual sense. (278, my italics)

The primordial *Logos* "is" Being itself "is" the One wherein and whereby All beings come-to-pass. Therefore, as he observes, "logic" must now be understood as "the meditation on 'the *Logos*,' as Being itself offers itself to be known originarily and in this way reveals itself as the primordial to-be-thought" (278). Moreover, as he continues, meditating on this primordial "logic" opens up for us the opportunity "to learn to experience [again] the genuine to-be-thought, Being itself" and to preserve and nurture this "relation" with Being (278). To restore our bond with Being offers the possibility of a radical rethinking of ourselves and a radical transformation in our way of being (*Wesenswandlung*). With moving and compelling language, he points out the existential significance of our recovery of the *experience* of Being as the *Logos*:

> This more primordial logic, as the meditation on the primordial essence of the *Logos*, is basically without a body of knowledge; it is poor compared with the abundance of learnable propositions and cognitional skills of metaphysical logic, its systematics and its series of theories. This more primordial logic is only the unabating practice of, or really only the preparation for, taking [*tun*] a simple step of thinking into the region of the genuinely to-be-thought. The more primordial logic thus intended is concerned with this "doing" [*Tun*], which is at the same time a "letting," namely, *to let Being essence* [*wesen*] *from out of its own truth*. (279; my italics)

III.   The Human Being's *logos* as *homologein* in Relation to the "Saying" of the Primordial *Logos*

"The human being himself must then as the being that he is, in the core of his essence, 'have' a *logos*, which, as this *logos*, is 'the relation' [*die Beziehung*] to the *Logos* in the sense of the

Being of beings" (294). Heidegger's position that the human being cor-responds to and with the primordial *Logos* (Being) is generally known (although not very much attended to in recent years), but there are several interesting particulars in the lecture course that we do not find in the more commonly read essay from 1951.

The theme and imagery of "breathing in and out" (*Einatmen/Ausatmen*) play a prominent role only in the lecture course. When Heidegger turns his attention to the human being, who has a distinctive relation to the *Logos* (279), he begins by observing that the human is a *zoon*, a *Lebewesen*, a "living being" (280). He inquires further into the proper meaning of "living," the Greek word *zoe*. He notes that for the Greeks, *zoe* was understood in the same manner as *physis*, that is, as the emerging-from-out-of-itself that is at the same time a going-back-into-itself. From ancient times, we have called the distinctive mark or feature of life and of all living things *psyche* or "soul" (*Seele*), and all living things have been said to be "besouled" or "ensouled" (*Beseelte*). *Psyche* or the soul signifies "breath," he continues, and I think it is significant that he uses both the word *der Atem* and the more spiritual/poetic word *der Hauch* to name "breath" (280). The "breath" he is speaking about, he states, is not to be understood simply in the narrow sense of "air" as it is related to "the functioning of the organs of respiration," but he does not clarify the broader, richer sense of "breath" that he is suggesting. He allows the word "breath" to resonate ("to breathe," we might also say in English).

Nevertheless, he maintains that this phenomenon of "breathing in" and "breathing out" is indeed related to the whole "essence" of all living things, although it is not the breathing in and out of air as such (as this is carried on by the respiratory systems of certain living creatures) that is the essential matter. Rather, it is the rhythm of "reaching out" (*ausholen*) into the Open and "bringing back" (*einholen*) from the Open (while always remaining in the Open) that is "the fundamental feature" of all that is living. In fact, this dynamic, rhythmic "reaching out" and "bringing back" must be considered the mark of *everything* that is insofar as everything belongs within the unfolding of *physis*. Therefore,

Heidegger concludes – somewhat surprisingly, perhaps, but also most poetically – that *everything that is* "lives" (*lebt*) and in a certain sense is "ensouled" (281).

There is, perhaps, an element of "Nature mysticism" (or *physis*-mysticism) in these reflections, and understandably it is not for all philosophical tastes. Nonetheless, this is precisely the kind of resonant reflection that is distinctively Heideggerian, and some patience is needed in order to appreciate what he is seeing in his saying. But, first, to continue, he proceeds to mark out how the human being, among beings, is to be understood along these lines. Again, all things, everything, may be said to be *zoe* and *psyche* insofar as they are enfolded in the unfolding of Being-*physis*-the primordial *Logos* and therein pulsate within the Open. He adds, though, that some beings may have "*logos*," and this means that some beings have a distinctive and special relation to the Open wherein the "reaching out" and "bringing back" is to be thought specifically in terms of a "gleaning" (*lesen*) or "gathering" (*sammeln*) (281). Such are the "living beings" of the kind (*Art*) that is the human being, and this "*legein*" of the human being is called *homologein* in the saying of Heraclitus. Consequently, according to Heidegger, "This one that emerges and thus this one that essences, the human being, is open to the *Logos*" (281), and "the depth of the human *logos* consists in the relation of this [human] *logos* to *the Logos*" (323). "The" *Logos* is the primordial fore-gathering, which, as he explicitly states, is Being itself (*das Sein selbst*, 319).

This is all somewhat difficult and obscure, admittedly, but let us consider more carefully what he has "gathered" with his words. It is apparent that he is offering a richly poetical philosophical account of all-that-is. We discern in what he is saying his fundamental understanding of Being-*physis*-Nature as the one-and-only, temporal-spatial unfolding of all beings and things. All things (*panta*) emerge out of, issue forth from, the One (*hen*), but, assuredly, the One (Being) is no "being," no "principle," apart from the Many. Indeed, at a later point in the lecture course he is at pains to say that although there is most certainly a "relation" (*Bezug, Beziehung*) between the *legein* of the human being and the primordial *Logos*, this is not to be understood in any traditional philosophical or theological sense as a "relation" of a wholly independent entity to another (327–33).

All beings, in their own particular way, have this relation-as-belonging to the primordial *Logos* that lays them out and gathers them. In this way, according to his vision, all beings, including human beings in a special manner, move along the Way as "reaching out and bringing back" within the Open/Way (Being-*physis*-*Logos*). This dynamic of "reaching out / bringing back" (*ausholen*/*einholen*) that he describes has several dimensions, but we may observe more broadly that this motif points to and points out once again (but in a novel way) his abiding insight into the way of all things, that is to say: All beings are on the way as they are moved along by the Being-way, and along their own way, at the heart of their wayfaring, is this perpetual, rhythmic flowing "out and in" within the primordial "out and in" of the Being-way itself. All things – the tree, the stone, the cabin; the flower, the child, the basket – all things "breathing" in their own way within the "breathing" of the Being-way itself. Alas, I suppose that one either "sees" this along with Heidegger, or one does not. Nevertheless, we might keep in mind that "breath" and "breathing" have for millennia been mythologized and poetized in terms of a "life force" that courses and pulses through all things, and Heidegger's particular version of this in the lecture course taps into this rich and long-standing "spiritual" – or poetical – way of seeing. So, for example, among the many voices in this tradition, we hear Walt Whitman singing, "Smile O voluptuous cool-breath'd earth!"[3]

Yet to continue, what additionally can we say about the *homologein* that is proper to the human being? How does the human being "gather" in relation to the primordial "fore-gathering"? According to Heidegger as he translates and reads fragment 50, which I laid out earlier, Heraclitus tells us that for us to truly "gather," which is "knowing," we must be able to "hearken" (*horchen*) in humble silence (*gehorsam*, obediently) to the primordial *Logos* and what it "says." In fact, he states that Heraclitus is emphatic that we are called, in the first place, to listen and hearken to the saying of the *Logos*, and *not* (the "sharp *ouk*," he points out, that begins the fragment) to the voice and speech of the human being (243–4). Furthermore, Heidegger boldly maintains that the *Logos* is "indeed a kind of saying [*Sagen*] and word [*Wort*]" (259) and also "a kind of speech [*Rede*] and voice [*Stimme*]" (244), yet to be perfectly clear, the *Logos* is "*manifestly not the voice of a human being*" (244, my italics).

I shall say more about the "saying" of the *Logos* in a moment, but I note that this matter for thought is intimately related to how *physis* "gives signs," which was discussed at length in the previous chapter. First, however, his understanding of humble and silent "hearkening" to the primordial *Logos* (Being) deserves a few additional words.

With the emergence of philosophical "Hermeneutics" as a discipline of study in the latter part of the twentieth century (based on the philosophical work of Hans-Georg Gadamer and others), it has become commonplace to maintain that "dialogue" and "discourse" with other human beings in the pursuit of "understanding" is the central human activity. Furthermore, it is generally maintained that this philosophical perspective is a development out of Heidegger's own thinking. This is understandable, but there is also something off the mark about this claim. No doubt, Heidegger's deep concern with "language" is central to the development of these hermeneutical perspectives, but if we consider the matter more carefully, we realize that his fundamental orientation or point of departure is quite different from that of Hermeneutics.

Hermeneutical thinking in general is focused on the human being "hearkening" to other human beings and engaging in "dialogue," in good faith, in the pursuit of a (finite and fragile) shared understanding. Yet Heidegger is clear in this lecture course (and in many other places) that our *legein*, our "gathering" (the "knowing" and "wisdom" spoken of in Heraclitus's sayings), is first and foremost a matter of the silent (and obedient) hearkening to "the voice" *of Being* as the primordial *Logos*, "the primordial fore-gathering" (242–6, 383). It would seem, then, that from his perspective the primary focus in Hermeneutics on "dialogue" among human beings (as constitutive and important as this surely is) is misplaced because such conversation cannot have the proper depth and discovery unless we have first listened attentively to the "saying" of the Being-way itself. It is our attunement to Being that matters in the first place, and – let us put this plainly – this does not *require* social or communal discourse. As he remarks in the lecture course, our "highest possible relation" is with Being, a relation that "grounds all other human relations to human beings and to things" (294). For the later Heidegger in particular, the rich solitude of silent listening to Being-*physis-Logos* as it unfolds is the primary way. Yet paradoxically, it is also the way that leads to perhaps the richest kind of community – the "community" of *all* mortals and beings and things as they come forth from out of the Being-way and go forth the same way. Arriving, lingering, departing; everything "breathing in and out." We might add, and only gently so, that this meditative way appears to be increasingly lost or forgotten in the contemporary world, not only in our intensely "connected" culture, but also in the various recent versions of hermeneutical thinking that focus almost exclusively on the linguistic, the social, and the political.

In the lecture course, he is also clear that his understanding of "the primordial *Logos*" has nothing to do with the age-old Christian onto-theological notion of the "Word" (*Logos, Verbum*), which is God in the figure of Christ, the second person of the Trinity (331). Accordingly, what he means by humbly hearkening to the *Logos* has little to do with any traditional "religious" practice of scrupulously attending to a supreme "transcendent" deity. We may, however, move closer to Heidegger's way of thinking by considering the ways of those who have been imbued with a deep reverence for Nature, someone like the great American naturalist John Muir:

> When one is alone at night in the depths of these woods, the stillness is at once awful and sublime. Every leaf seems to speak.[4]

Every leaf seems to speak. In stillness, we "hear" the leaf and the flower, the wind and the rain, the sun and the moon "speaking." Muir's words resonate with us, but more often than not our way to a fuller understanding and appreciation of them is blocked because we are so accustomed in the contemporary world to think that the human being is the source and measure of all "saying." Heidegger's meditations on the primordial *Logos* boldly challenge this assumption. In other words, Being as the *Logos* is the "saying" – "word," "speech," "voice" – precisely as the laying out, opening up, showing, shining-forth of all that is. The *Logos* "addresses" us first, "appeals," "calls" to us in the first place. This primordial "saying" as "fore-gathering," which he identifies with the Greek word *gnome* (the to-be-known) of Heraclitus's fragments 41 and 78, is "not of human origin," he insists (351). Rather, it is proper for us only to "gather" from within the "fore-gathering." "The human *logos* is the relation to Being, to the *Logos*" (358), and in this relation our "gathering" is *homologein*, that is, a *cor-respondence* to and with the primordial *legein*. Heidegger returns to fragment 112 to say more about this correspondence:

> *to phronein arete megiste, kai sophin alethea legein kai poiein kata phusin epaiontas*

This fragment, in both German and English, is generally translated along the lines of "Thinking well is the greatest excellence; and wisdom is to act and speak what is true, perceiving things according to their nature." For Heidegger, all such translations miss what is essential, so he first inquires into the words "*alethea legein*" of the fragment and considers the connection that Heraclitus makes between "*alethea*" (the accusative case) and "*legein*." The Greek word *alethea* originally meant "the true" (*das Wahre*) but in the sense of "what is unconcealed," what "appears," what "shines forth," what is "manifest." (247–8; 359–70). His point is that "the true" (*alethea*) is, principally and primarily, what shows itself from itself, and not any kind of statement or proposition. We have come across this reading many times before, of course, but here Heidegger wishes to show that the *legein* of the human being is a "gathering" and "preserving" of what is "unconcealed" and, therefore, that "genuine" "knowing" (*phronein; Wissen*) and wisdom (*sophia*) is precisely this "gathering unto unconcealedness" (364). Human *legein* gathers what is fore-gathered by the primordial *Logos* and makes manifest what is manifest from out of primordial *Aletheia*. Thus, *Logos* and *Aletheia* belong together; they are "the same." Being as *Aletheia* as the primordial *Logos* is the "saying" that speaks to us precisely in its unfolding and laying out and laying open all that is, and we "gather" in word what is addressed to us (as *wordable*). *Every leaf seems to speak.*

Yet such human "gathering" was not only called *legein* by the Greeks but *poiein* as well. Heraclitus's fragment 112 speaks of *legein* in relation to what is true (*alethea*) and of *poiein* in relation to *physis* (*poiein kata physin*). *Poiein* is a making manifest as a "bringing forth" (*Hervorbringen*) in accordance with the primordial bringing forth that is *physis* – but *physis* is the "measure" (*Maβ*), Heidegger insists, and not the subjective designs and dictates of the human subject who "produces" things (367). It is along with, in accordance with, *physis* that the sculptor "brings forth" the "look of the god" from the block of marble (366), and his point here reminds us of the words of the American architect Louis Kahn, who was fond of saying that the practice of architecture is fundamentally a matter of asking the bricks and stones what they want to be. All "art," Heidegger continues, is in "the highest sense" this kind of "bringing forth" in accordance with the arising-emerging that is Beyng (*Seyn*) as *physis* (369). "Art" is never merely "made"; it is brought forth and gathered from out of the emerging. Therefore, *legein* and *poiein*, what he refers to as fundamental "thinking" (*Denken*) and "poetizing" (*Dichten*), although not "identical," are the "same" as the two distinctive ways that the human being cor-responds (*homologein*) to Being as the primordial *Logos*, *Aletheia*, *Physis* (370). We human beings "know" and are "wise" only to the extent that we humbly hearken to the "saying" of the primordial *Logos*. His "translation" of fragment 112 thus reads: "Meditative thinking is the highest nobleness, and this is so because knowing is: to gather what is unconcealed (from out of concealment and for this concealment) in the [manner of] bringing forth in accordance with emerging – (and yet all of this) in hearkening to the primordial fore-gathering" (373–4).

Heidegger sums up these reflections in a concise statement that yet one more time elucidates and affirms the structural priority – the primacy – of Being in relation to the human being:

> *Aletheia, Physis, Logos* are *the Same* [Heidegger's emphasis], not in the empty uniformity of the coincidence in the identical undifferentiated, but rather as the primordial self-gathering-together in the One that is rich with distinction: *to Hen*. The *Hen*, the primordially unifying One and Only, is the *Logos* as the *Aletheia* as the *Physis*. To this One, to be thought in this way, to the *Logos*, corresponds, in *homologein* and as *homologein*, every human *legein* that reaches out and brings back; *legein*, which is itself at the same time *poiein* – bringing forth. Yet both [*legein* and *poiein*] are in the manner of the hearkening gleaning of the gathered self-gathering unto the primordial fore-gathering. (371)

Concluding Thought

This 1944 lecture course was among Heidegger's richest and most engaging. My aim has been to get into view certain fresh features of his understanding of the sayings of Heraclitus, and to show thereby that what mattered most to Heidegger in reading Heraclitus was *the recovery of the experience of Being itself*. With demanding but compelling language, Heidegger reminds us that we exist in "relation" to Being and that in this ek-static relation we ceaselessly "reach out" (*aussholen*) unto Being and "bring back" (*einholen*) in the *word* what is addressed to us by Being itself as the primordial *Logos*. Although he does not mention this (and perhaps surprisingly so), the German word he employs, *einholen*, is often used in speaking of fishermen, who having cast their nets upon the sea then "draw (them) back" (*einholen*) laden with a multitude of fish. This image is fitting. Our *logos* is always "cast out" unto the *Logos*, and we "draw back" what has been "fore-gathered" in a multitude of words. Word upon word upon word – endlessly, abundantly, playfully, joyously – but never are we able to exhaust the inexhaustible "saying" of Being itself.

Afterword

around me surges a miracle of unceasing
birth and glory and death and resurrection

e.e. cummings[1]

Come forth, and bring with you a heart
That watches and receives.

William Wordsworth[2]

Heidegger's way of Being, the Being-way, is the way of *physis*,
aletheia, the primordial *Logos*, and the *hen* – but also the way of
Ereignis, *Es gibt*, and *Lichtung*. This has been brought into sharp
relief in the foregoing studies. It is rather puzzling, therefore,
that several contemporary Heidegger commentators have
turned away from his lifelong commitment to these *Ur*-words
of the earliest Greek thinkers; and puzzling, too, that they have
overlooked the clarity of his statements on *Ereignis*, *Es gibt*, and
Lichtung in relation to Being. With respect to these latter terms,
four statements by Heidegger, which I have highlighted and discussed along the way, must always be taken into account:

- "Yet the sole aim of this lecture has been to bring into view
  Being itself as *Ereignis*." (From "Time and Being")
- "But the clearing [*die Lichtung*] itself is Being." (From "Letter
  on Humanism")

- "For the 'it' [*es*] that here 'gives' [*gibt*] is Being itself." (From "Letter on Humanism")
- "It is a matter of understanding that the deepest meaning of Being is *letting*." (From the seminar in Le Thor, 11 September 1969)

In my view, all recent scholarly efforts to maintain that Heidegger subordinated *Sein* to *Ereignis* (or any other term) simply founder upon these firm statements. Being – also properly named Beyng, Being itself, Being as such, Being as Being – is the "same" as *Ereignis*, *Es gibt*, and *Lichtung*. There is also clear textual evidence that the matter is no different with another of his significant terms, *die Gegend* or *die Gegnet*. In the 1944 lecture course on Heraclitus that we examined in chapter 6, he comments that "the region" (*die Gegend*) – as also "the expanse" (*die Weite*) – in which all things "sojourn" and are "safeguarded" is the primordial *Logos* as Being itself.[3] Also closely related here is his emphatic statement in the Parmenides lecture course of 1942–3: *The Open is Being itself* (*Das Offene is das Sein selbst*).[4] Thus so many rich and resonant names for Being, and it is precisely this remarkable, even herculean, effort to think Being *as temporal opening, showing, shining-forth, manifestation* that marks the originality, distinctiveness, and compelling beauty of Heidegger's philosophical project in relation to Husserl's transcendental idealism and all other similar transcendental perspectives that are principally concerned with the constitution of meaning.

Yet all this said, let us keep in view that the studies in this volume have been concerned not only with clarifying the proper character of the Being-way, but also with clarifying *our* way in relation to the Being-way. We now see more clearly that Heidegger's way is indeed primarily a "meditative thinking," which, regrettably, is largely out of step with much of contemporary life, but which invites us, nonetheless, to enter into a deep, rich, serene contemplative and mindful comportment towards all beings and things in their temporal unfolding.[5] Upon awakening to the way of Being, we see with fresh eyes the emergence and shining-forth of all beings and things in their "truth" (chapter 1). We catch sight of the hidden "gleaming" stream that moves all things along (chapter 2). We are set free from our Cartesian ego-prisons to experience once more the immediacy and power of the presence of all beings and things (chapters 3 and 4). We are called upon to quiet ourselves and bring ourselves to stillness in order to listen, truly listen, to all that approaches and addresses us – and then to make a joyful noise to herald everything that is gathered before us (chapters 5 and 6). We are the "bearers of tidings" in the originary sense of this English expression. "Tiding" originally meant "a happening, an event, an occurrence," and we bear, we bring, to all – we announce – this most marvellous happening (*Ereignis*) of all beings and things.[6] The resounding of Being is resounded by us. And yet not *only* by us, it is reasonable to think.[7]

To recover what Heidegger calls "the experience of Being" is also for us to come to an appreciation of the ultimate simplicity and "lightness" of our own being. I have discussed at length the development and significance of his notion *die Lichtung* (the lighting/clearing) in *Engaging Heidegger*, but one point bears restating.[8] It appears that late in his thinking Heidegger learned that the German word *Lichtung* was derived not only from the word for shining "light" (*Licht*) – but also from the word *leicht*, "light" in the sense of "free and easy and unburdened." He subsequently overplayed this point in his linguistic analysis of the word *Lichtung* in his statements of the 1960s, but that aside, we can still appreciate why he found his discovery important.

To think Being as *die Lichtung* in terms of *leicht* is to be mindful of how all beings and things – including ourselves – are unencumbered, freed up, released, set free and set moving again. He was fond of referring to the German expression *den Anker lichten*, "to raise the anchor," because "*lichten*" here speaks to releasing the anchor "from the encompassing ocean floor and lifting it into the free of water and air."[9] In other words, for us to enter fully into the experience of Being is for us to free up our own being, to flow freely with all beings and things, to let go of the heavy weight of our "substantiality" and learn to pass "lightly" along the way of everything. Of course, this view is far removed from the "tragic vision" that has so dominated our cultural perspective for so long. Death, for example, our mortality, we come to see differently – not "tragic" in itself, not "evil" or "absurd," not a great enemy that must be overcome, conquered, defied. To embrace the Being-way is to embrace that we, like all beings, arrive, linger, and depart. We come-to-pass and we pass away. The joy is in our passing this way at all.

Heidegger's way of Being continues to challenge us to see our way of being in a new light – and to take it up with a new "lightness." But the task is not simply philosophical. It is more radical and far-reaching; it is to revision ourselves, our relations, our *ethos* in accordance with the Being-way.

Notes

Unless otherwise noted, all references to Heidegger's works are to the volumes in the *Gesamtausgabe* (*Complete Works*) published by Vittorio Klostermann, Frankfurt am Main. I cite GA followed by volume number and page number. Where appropriate, I also provide the corresponding reference in an available English translation. I have often modified the published English translations.

Introduction

1 Heinrich Petzet, *Encounters and Dialogues with Martin Heidegger, 1929–1976*, trans. Parvis Emad and Kenneth Maly (Chicago: University of Chicago Press, 1993), 127.
2 Richard Capobianco, *Engaging Heidegger* (Toronto: University of Toronto Press, 2010).
3 It is preferable, I think, to speak of the human being as *human Dasein* and not simply as *Dasein*. Even so, in the studies that follow, I use the word Dasein to refer specifically to the human being (*qua* human *ek-sistence*), as Heidegger was wont to do, especially in his early work. This has also become customary in the scholarly literature, so I follow the convention. Nevertheless, I am always mindful – and I ask the reader to be always mindful – that in his later reflections, Heidegger more commonly referred simply to "the human being" (*der Mensch*). Moreover, he sometimes employed the term Dasein in a broader and richer way that was more in keeping with his later focus on Being itself. For example, in his 1959 lecture "Hölderlin's Earth and Heaven"

(GA 4: 152–81), he refers to "heaven's manifestations" and mentions in particular *der Blitz*, the lightning-flash. The lightning-flash speaks most powerfully to how all beings and things temporally come-to-pass. Everything appears in a "flash," or in "the wink or gleam of an eye," we might say, and Heidegger himself states that *Blitz* is the same word as *Blick* (glance) (161). And he continues: "*Im Blick ist Dasein. Das Gewitter heisst darum das 'Daseyn Gottes'*" (161). That is: In the lightning-flash, in the flash or gleam of an eye, is *Dasein*. The thunderstorm is, in this way, "the *Daseyn* of god" (referring to a line from Hölderlin's poem "*Griechenland*"). Here, then, Heidegger allows the word Dasein to name a happening, showing, manifestation, coming-to-pass of what-is as it (eventfully) emerges from out of the temporal-spatial Being-way, or the "holy," as he refers to the *Ur*-phenomenon in this text. To be sure, there is something special about *human* Dasein (in the figure of the poet), but only insofar as the poet is the one who so exquisitely "allows to shine back" in language the radiance of the manifestations of heaven and earth – and the unique light of the manifesting-way itself (Being itself, the holy, *physis*-Nature). For more on this "unique light," see esp. ch. 2.

4   See the statements "*Aletheia* (Heraclitus, Fragment B 16)" and "*Logos* (Heraclitus, Fragment B 50)" in *Early Greek Thinking*, trans. David Farrell Krell and Frank A. Capuzzi (San Francisco: Harper & Row, 1984).

1. Reaffirming "The Truth of Being"

1   Thomas Sheehan has made the most concerted effort to argue for the pure transcendental reduction of (Heidegger's) *Sein* to *Sinn* (of Being to meaning or sense). See "A Paradigm Shift in Heidegger Research," *Continental Philosophy Review* 34 (2001): 183–202. See also, more recently, "Astonishing! Things Make Sense!," *Gatherings: The Heidegger Circle Annual* 1 (2011): 1–25. Related: Steven Galt Crowell, *Husserl, Heidegger, and the Space of Meaning* (Evanston: Northwestern University Press, 2001); Dan Zahavi, *Subjectivity and Selfhood* (Cambridge, MA: MIT Press, 2005); Burt Hopkins, *Intentionality in Husserl and Heidegger* (New York: Springer, 1993). My readings and reflections that follow in these studies are broadly mindful of all such strictly "transcendental–phenomenological" readings of Heidegger's core matter, and of Sheehan's reading in particular. Even so, I would

also make note that many years earlier, Hubert Dreyfus had laid out his basic reading of Heidegger that the source of the "sense" of things is to be found in Dasein's "absorbed," everyday, skilful coping practices; see his *Being-in-the-World: A Commentary on Heidegger's Being and Time, Division I* (Cambridge, MA: MIT Press, 1991). Related: William Blattner, *Heidegger's Being and Time: A Reader's Guide* (London: Continuum, 2006); Mark Okrent, *Heidegger's Pragmatism: Understanding, Being, and the Critique of Metaphysics* (Ithaca: Cornell University Press, 1991); Richard Rorty, "Heidegger, Contingency, and Pragmatism," in *Essays on Heidegger and Others: Philosophical Papers* (Cambridge: Cambridge University Press, 1991), 27–49. Sheehan and Dreyfus read Heidegger from within very different philosophical traditions, no doubt, but it remains, nonetheless, that for both the central matter of Heidegger's thinking concerns the human being – Dasein and Dasein's making "sense" of things.

2 See, for example, Heidegger's letter to Manfred Frings dated 20 October 1966 in *Heidegger and the Quest for Truth*, ed. Manfred Frings (Chicago: Quadrangle Books, 1968), 17–21. See also his Preface (1962) to William J. Richardson's *Heidegger: Through Phenomenology to Thought* (The Hague: Martinus Nijhoff, 1963/1974), xv: "the question of Being in the sense of the thinking of Being as such (the manifestness of Being)."

3 GA 15: 385–6; *Four Seminars*, trans. Andrew Mitchell and François Raffoul (Bloomington: Indiana University Press, 2003), 72.

4 §13–15 in GA 56/57: 63–76; *Towards the Definition of Philosophy*, trans. Ted Sadler (London: Athlone Press, 2008), 51–60.

5 For the German word *welten*, see the entry in the *Deutsches Wörterbuch* by Jacob Grimm and Wilhelm Grimm, vol. 28 at 1563. For *world* as a verb in English, see the entry "world, v." in the *Oxford English Dictionary*. Consider as well how this reading helps us understand his many later statements regarding "world," such as from 1941–2: "The springing up of the world comes to pass as the self-opening … The opening is *aletheia*; it is unconcealedness, truth" (GA 88: 325). And in his many readings of Heraclitus from the early 1940s onward, "world," properly understood as the Heraclitean *kosmos*, is another name for Being, and world/*kosmos*/Being is that which "shimmers ungraspably throughout everything." GA 15: 282; *Four Seminars*, 8.

6 I examine the central importance of the image of the "sun" and "light" for the early and middle Heidegger in my *Engaging*

Heidegger, chs. 5 and 6. Apart from the texts, another clue is to be found in Heidegger's famous hut in Todtnauberg. In Adam Sharr's *Heidegger's Hut* (Cambridge, MA: MIT Press, 2006), there is a lovely photo of Heidegger, reposed and pensive, sitting at the head of the dining table (33). To the left of him, as if an honoured guest at his table, is a great smiling sun that is carved into the wood of the inside back of a chair. Heidegger's "sun": the enabling light that allows all things to appear – Being itself! The trope of "light" (*lumen, lux*) became more problematical to Heidegger in the later years because of the Platonic/metaphysical overtones; still, it remained a central feature of his thinking of Being from start to finish (see ch. 2).

7   Martin Heidegger, *"Die Grundfrage nach dem Sein selbst"* ("The Fundamental Question Concerning Being Itself") *Heidegger Studies* 2 (1986): 1–3. Note that Heidegger clearly refers to the question of *Sein selbst* (Being itself) as the *Grundfrage* (the *fundamental* question). In contrast, the *Leitfrage* (the *guiding* question) is Heidegger's term for the inquiry into *Seiendheit* (beingness), the beingness of a being, which in his view was primarily pursued in the metaphysical tradition of thinking from the very beginning. I maintain that Sheehan's reading of the *Grundfrage* is at odds with Heidegger's own many statements on the matter, such as this one. Furthermore, Heidegger's synoptic statement here gives us an indication of why even in his earliest work he did not focus on Husserl's key notion of "constitution." That is, we might say that Heidegger's focal point was always the manifestness of Being – and the manifestness of Being is *structurally* prior to, and the ontological condition of, any such "constitution" of meaning. Being is not reducible to meaning, and this is elucidated further in the following chapters.

8   GA 15: 345; *Four Seminars*, 47.

9   GA 15: 334–5; *Four Seminars*, 40–1.

10   GA 54; GA 55; GA 9.

11   GA 27: 78 (my translation; no available English translation). See also in the same volume, 104–5. Heidegger, in maintaining that it is the being itself that is manifest, uses the phrase *an ihm selbst* rather than *an sich selbst*. This way of phrasing the matter appears to enable him (1) to draw a clear contrast with

the Kantian/Neo-Kantian *Ding an sich* and (2) to emphasize that it is the being in *it* itself that is "true." Heidegger also often employed the phrase *von sich her* – a manifestation or showing of the being *from itself forth*; see, for example, the 1969 seminar in Le Thor in GA 15: 326–9, where he also characterizes the being "in its place" (*in seiner Lage*) as "it lets itself be seen" (327). Note that this instructive phrase "*in seiner Lage*" is omitted in the English edition, *Four Seminars*, 35. See also ch. 3.

12 Heidegger's culminating statement on this Aristotelian text can be found in his 1930 summer semester lecture course in GA 31. See especially §9(c), (d), and (e): 80–109. *The Essence of Human Freedom*, trans. Ted Sadler (London: Athlone Press, 2005), 56–74.

13 GA 23 (no available English translation); specifically §10–15: 41–68. For Heidegger's exchange with Scheler in 1924, see "Being-there and Being-true According to Aristotle" in *Becoming Heidegger*, ed. Theodore Kisiel and Thomas Sheehan (Evanston: Northwestern University Press, 2007), 233.

14 Thomas Aquinas, *Quaestiones Disputatae*, vol. 1, *De Veritate*, ed. P. Fr. Raymundi Spiazzi, O.P. (Rome: Marietti Editori, 1953), 3.

15 "Plato's Doctrine of Truth," in *Pathmarks*, ed. William McNeill (Cambridge: Cambridge University Press, 1998), 182 (marginal note a); GA 9: 237. Also consider a marginal note he made concerning Thomas in the text of the 1949 "Introduction to 'What is Metaphysics?'": "*Veritas* in Thomas Aquinas always *in intellectu*, [even] be it the *intellectus divinus*." In *Pathmarks*, 280 (marginal note c); GA 9: 369. I also note that this original and distinctive position that Heidegger maintains time and time again – Being as *Aletheia*, Being is *Aletheia* – is altogether missed by Sheehan in his readings of Heidegger. For Sheehan, Heidegger's *aletheia* pertains to the human being only; see, for example, his "Astonishing!," 10–11. Yet again, let us keep Heidegger's distinctive position always in view: "Being is *the* truth as such" (GA 73.1: 133, his italics).

16 Heidegger, "On the Question Concerning the Determination of the Matter for Thinking," trans. Richard Capobianco and Marie Göbel, *Epoché* 14, no. 2 (Spring 2010): 213–23. GA 16: 620–33, but see our preface to the translation for a complete provenance.

17 Heidegger, "On the Question," 219–20. For a discussion of Heidegger's special use of the word *glänzen*, see ch. 2.

18 Consider the clarity and force of Heidegger's position as stated in
    "Plato's Doctrine of Truth" (composed 1940): "Unconcealedness
    reveals itself … as the fundamental feature of beings themselves."
    And further: "As Plato conceives it, unconcealedness remains
    harnessed in a relation to looking, apprehending, thinking, and
    asserting. To follow this relation means *to relinquish the essence of
    unconcealedness*" (my emphasis). In *Pathmarks*, 182. GA 9: 237–8. See
    also the *Parmenides* volume, GA 54: 50: "Nevertheless, for the Greeks,
    and still for Aristotle, *aletheia* is the character of beings and not only a
    character of the perceiving of beings and of statements about them."
19 GA 15: 327; *Four Seminars*, 35. Wittgenstein's opening proposition
    in the *Tractatus* is generally translated as "The world is all that is
    the case."
20 "The Fundamental Question Concerning Being Itself," 1, my italics.
21 GA 88: 205 (my translation, no available English translation; my
    italics).
22 GA 88: 311.
23 GA 77: 147 (italics mine, except for the last line).
24 GA 10: 103; *The Principle of Reason*, trans. Reginald Lilly
    (Bloomington: Indiana University Press, 1991), 70.
25 GA 15: 345; *Four Seminars*, 47.
26 These texts and other similar texts explicitly state or strongly suggest
    that Being and its "truth" "is" even if the human being is not; they
    also clearly speak to the trajectory of his thinking after *Being and
    Time*. See also Heidegger's own *retractatio* of his early position in
    Being and Time in the "Letter on Humanism," *Pathmarks*, 256–7; GA
    9: 336–7. The first and second lines cited are from "Recollection in
    Metaphysics"/"*Die Erinnerung in die Metaphysik*" (1941). GA 6.2:
    441, 447, my italics. Cf. Joan Stambaugh's translation in the volume
    The End of Philosophy (Chicago: University of Chicago Press, 2003),
    76, 82. The third line is from a text included as an Addendum in the
    Parmenides volume (lecture course 1942–3), GA 54: 249. The German
    reads "*Nur weil das Sein und die Wahrheit des Seins wesentlich is über
    alle Menschen und Menschentümer hinweg.*" The word *Menschentum*
    is commonly translated as "humanity," but Heidegger uses the
    plural (rare), which would be oddly translated as "humanities," as
    Schuwer and Rojcewicz do in *Parmenides* (Bloomington: Indiana
    University Press, 1992), 166. Consequently, I have opted for "every

historical people" or "all historical peoples." The fourth line is also from the *Parmenides* volume, GA 54: 164; *Parmenides,* 111. The fifth line is from the 1943 lecture course on Heraclitus, GA 55: 166. Also with respect to this line, see the seminar in Le Thor in 1966 (9 September), where Heidegger restated the view that *physis* and *Logos* and *kosmos* spoken of by Heraclitus say the same as Being. Commenting on fragment 30, he observed: "*kosmos* [is] older than the gods and human beings, who remain related back to it, *since not the gods or human beings could ever have brought it [kosmos] forth.*" GA 15: 282; *Four Seminars,* 8; my italics.

27 See especially Heidegger's 1955–6 lecture course "*Der Satz vom Grund*," GA 10, translated as *The Principle of Reason* (cited above).

28 In this regard, note Heidegger's remark in Le Thor in 1969: "We must never allow ourselves to lose sight of the fact that the determinations of *phainesthai* and of the [*on hos*] *alethes* are fully present in the Platonic *eidos*." GA 15: 333–4; *Four Seminars,* 40. See also my remarks in ch. 3.

29 *Engaging Heidegger,* ch. 1.

30 *Engaging Heidegger,* ch. 6.

31 *Engaging Heidegger,* chs. 2, 5, 6.

32 See *Engaging Heidegger,* 43–7. For Heidegger's characterization of *Ereignis* as "the most gentle of all laws," see GA 12: 248. Richard Polt, although not making the same point as I am here, nonetheless takes note of the connection to the early 1919 seminar in his careful study "*Ereignis,*" in *A Companion to Heidegger,* ed. Hubert L. Dreyfus and Mark Wrathall (Oxford: Blackwell, 2005), 375–91.

33 See especially Heidegger's 1957 lecture "The Principle of Identity," in *Identity and Difference,* trans. Joan Stambaugh (New York: Harper & Row, 1969), 36.

34 GA 14: 26; *On Time and Being,* trans. Joan Stambaugh (Chicago: University of Chicago Press, 1972), 21. See *Engaging Heidegger,* 47–50.

35 GA 9: 334: "*Denn das 'es,' was hier 'gibt,' ist das Sein selbst.*" *Pathmarks,* 254–5.

36 *Engaging Heidegger,* chs. 5, 6.

37 GA 9: 332; *Pathmarks,* 253.

38 "On the Question Concerning the Determination of the Matter for Thinking," 221.

39 *Zollikoner Seminare,* ed. Medard Boss (Frankfurt am Main: Vittorio
    Klostermann, 1987/2006), 223. *Zollikon Seminars,* trans. Franz Mayr
    and Richard Askay (Evanston: Northwestern University Press,
    2001), 178 (translation slightly modified). Such texts are plainly
    at odds with Sheehan's repeated claim – a claim that is central in
    his "new paradigm" – that, for Heidegger, the human being is the ·
    whole of the clearing; see, for example, his "A Paradigm Shift,"
    193, and "Astonishing!," 9. Furthermore, in this same passage,
    Heidegger refers to Dasein as the guardian "of the *Ereignis.*"
    According to Heidegger, then, Dasein is the guardian of Being,
    Lichtung, and *Ereignis,* and thus we have additional reason to state
    that Being, *Lichtung, Ereignis* say "the same" – and additional
    reason to question Sheehan's reading of *Ereignis* as reducible to the
    human being's thrownness or finitude.
40 GA 15: 386–7; *Four Seminars,* 73.
41 GA 55: 371 (my translation; no available English translation).
42 GA 9: 239–301; *Pathmarks,* 183–230.
43 GA 55: 175 (my translation; no available English translation).
    The first epigraph that opens this essay is found within this
    passage. Heidegger's two brilliant lecture courses on Heraclitus
    that comprise GA 55 (first published in 1979) have not yet been
    translated into English in complete form. For a further discussion
    of these important texts with a focus on the matter of Being in
    relation to the human being, see chs. 5 and 6. Consider, too,
    Heidegger's equally clear and firm statement in his 1955–6
    lecture course "On the Principle of Ground": "Self-revealing is a
    fundamental feature of Being" (GA 10: 102).
44 The opening lines from Whitman's poem "A Song of the Rolling
    Earth."
45 GA 55: 179: "The *physis* itself is the self-showing that essentially
    shows itself in the signs." See also ch. 5.
46 GA 15: 403; *Four Seminars,* 94.

2. On Hölderlin on "Nature's Gleaming"

1 *"Das Glänzen der Natur ist Höheres Erscheinen"* in GA 75: 205–9.
   The editor, Curd Ochwadt, indicates that the text can be dated to
   "nach Juli 1970," but he also notes that this does not necessarily

refer to the second half of the year 1970 (see 394 and 398–9).
All translations by Richard Capobianco and Marie Göbel, and I
extend my heartfelt thanks to Marie Göbel for her collaboration.
Although the translations of Hölderlin's poems cited are our own
(and more suited to Heidegger's readings of these poems), we
have nonetheless consulted Michael Hamburger's elegant (but
considerably freer) translations in his *Friedrich Hölderlin: Poems
and Fragments* (London: Anvil Press Poetry, 2007), which includes
all the cited poetic lines except the final poem, *"Die Aussicht"* ("The
View").

2 From his Black Forest *Hütte* in October 1966, Heidegger wrote a
heartfelt sixtieth birthday greeting to Hannah Arendt upon her
entering the "autumn" of her life, and he included a copy of this
poem with his letter. *Martin Heidegger and Hannah Arendt, Briefe
1925 bis 1975* (Frankfurt am Main: Vittorio Klostermann, 1998),
153–4. Not long after, he also mentioned this poem to his friend
the clergyman Paul Hassler in a letter in the spring of 1967. In part,
Heidegger writes to Hassler, who had been ill: "Above all, I wish
that, in this period of recovery, undisguised nature addresses you
and that through nature you are claimed by what never ceases
to claim human beings. In one of Hölderlin's poems, composed
a year before his death, we read '*Das Glänzen der Natur ist höheres
Erscheinen*.' In view of these words, the talk about Hölderlin's
madness becomes puzzling." Heinrich Petzet, *Encounters and
Dialogues with Martin Heidegger, 1929–1976*, trans. Parvis Emad and
Kenneth Maly (Chicago: University of Chicago Press, 1993), 127
(but I have omitted their interpolated translation of Hölderlin's
verse line).

3 See especially his comment in Le Thor on 6 September 1969 in
GA 15: 346; in translation, *Four Seminars*, trans. Andrew Mitchell
and François Raffoul (Bloomington: Indiana University Press,
2003), 48 (slightly modified): "all our considerations spring
from a fundamental distinction that can be expressed thusly:
Being is not a being. This is the *ontological difference* (*ontologische
Differenz*, his italics) … Why is the ontological difference not able
to become a theme for metaphysics? Because if this were the case,
the ontological difference would be a being and no longer the
difference (*der Unterschied*) between Being and beings." See also

his comment on 5 September 1968 in GA 15: 310 and discussed in *Engaging Heidegger*, 17.

4 See also *Engaging Heidegger*, chs. 3 and 4.

5 *Engaging Heidegger*, 81–2, 159.

6 We find one such comment in the protocol for the last seminar at Zähringen on 8 September 1973, GA 15: 399. Yet here, too, it is perfectly clear that Heidegger means that Being as "presencing itself" as *aletheia* "shows itself" – *manifests itself* – in a different way from "beings" and that, therefore, a "phenomenology of the inapparent" is needed. See also ch. 5 for my discussion of this same point made by the "middle" Heidegger.

7 See, for example, his special use of *glänzen* in his 1965 address "On the Question Concerning the Determination of the Matter for Thinking," trans. Richard Capobianco and Marie Göbel, *Epoché* 14, no. 2 (2010): 219–20. See also ch. 1 for a discussion of a key passage from this text. In his reading of Hölderlin's poems, which we are discussing in this chapter, both "gleaming" and "golden" refer to the unique "shining-forth" of Nature (Being itself). The "higher revealing" of Nature is the shining that *allows* all other beings to shine forth. This is precisely the sense that Heidegger found in the word "gold" (in its "gleaming") in his elucidation of the first few lines of Pindar's *Isthmian Ode 5* in an undelivered lecture course on the saying of Anaximander that was most likely composed in 1942. This text has only recently been published in 2010, GA 78, *Der Spruch des Anaximander*, 67–94 and 285–96. In his excursus, Heidegger reads "gold" as that which "in its gleaming thus shining" lights up all other beings, that is, allows all other beings to shine forth, appear, come-to-presence (72–3). Thus, he states, "gold" is "in a certain manner" another name for Being itself (74) as this was glimpsed by the poet Pindar.

8 "O sweet spontaneous/ earth," e.e. cummings was moved to exclaim. "The very heart-gladness of the earth going on forever," John Muir marvelled. What Heidegger saw so clearly and vividly – the unceasing emerging and arising that is *physis* – poets and writers have well understood and celebrated in their own way. *E.E. Cummings: Selected Poems*, ed. Richard S. Kennedy (New York: Liveright Press, 1994), 18–19. *John of the Mountains: The Unpublished Journals of John Muir*, ed. Linnie Marsh Wolfe (Madison: University of Wisconsin Press, 1979), 233.

9 Heidegger also cited this poem in full at the conclusion of his 1951 lecture "... Poetically Man Dwells ..." GA 7: 208. Albert Hofstader offers a translation of the poem as part of his translation of the lecture in *Poetry, Language, Thought* (New York: Harper & Row, 1971), 229. Our translation is especially mindful of Heidegger's elucidations in the present piece.

3. The "Greek Experience" of Nature–*Physis*–Being

1 "Time and Being," trans. Joan Stambaugh, in *On Time and Being* (New York: Harper & Row, 1972), 21, 24. GA 14: 26, 29. See also *Engaging Heidegger*, 47–50. Note: In all citations that follow, italics are Heidegger's unless otherwise noted.

2 *Four Seminars*, trans. Andrew Mitchell and François Raffoul (Bloomington: Indiana University Press, 2003), 59. All further references in the essay are to the English translation, sometimes slightly modified. GA 15: 363.

3 GA 54: 212 (my italics).

4 Heidegger, "On the Question Concerning the Determination of the Matter for Thinking," trans. Richard Capobianco and Marie Göbel, *Epoché* 14, no. 2 (2010), 216. GA 16: 624.

5 *Hannah Arendt–Martin Heidegger Briefe 1925–1975* (Frankfurt am Main: Vittorio Klostermann, 2002), 153. *Letters 1925–1975, Hannah Arendt and Martin Heidegger*, trans. Andrew Shields (Orlando: Harcourt, 2004), 127 (slightly modified).

6 Martin Heidegger, "Preface," in William J. Richardson, *Heidegger: Through Phenomenology to Thought* (The Hague: Martinus Nijhoff, 1963/1974), xix (my emphasis).

7 For further consideration of this crucial point, see ch. 1. Consider, too, Heidegger's statement in his 1938 "The Age of the World Picture" (GA 5: 90–1): "[The human being's] receiving/taking-in [*das Vernehmen*] of beings [*Seienden*] belongs to Being [*Sein*] because it is from Being that it is demanded and determined. The being is that which emerges and opens itself; that which, as what is present, comes upon the human being that is present, that is, upon him who opens himself to what is present and thereby receives it. The being is not in being [*seiend*] by virtue of the human being looking upon it ... Rather, the human being is the one who is looked upon by beings, the one who is gathered by self-opening beings into presencing

along with them … The Greek human being *is* as the receiver [*der Vernehmer*] of beings." This is a slightly modified translation from *Off the Beaten Track*, trans. Julian Young and Kenneth Haynes (Cambridge: Cambridge University Press, 2002), 68.

8 GA 75: 249–73. My translation; no published English translation available.

9 From *Idyll 7*. Heidegger cites a German translation by Horst Rüdiger; this English translation is by Anthony Verity, *Theocritus Idylls* (London: Oxford University Press, 2003), 28–9.

10 Regarding these verse lines by Theocritus, Heidegger notes: "According to the report of the scholars, here may be composed, among all the Greek poems, the most *'Naturstimmung'* [in tune with nature] in the modern sense. The fading away of the mythical experience of the world probably freed up the presence of nature so described in the verses; [but this presence of nature is] much less or absolutely not a subjective experience in the modern sense" (269–70).

11 *Four Seminars*, 38; GA 15: 331.

12 William Wordsworth, "A Night-Piece": "and the vault, / Built round by those white clouds, enormous clouds, / Still deepens its unfathomable depth." The lines by e.e. cummings are from the second stanza of his poem "life is more true than reason will deceive." See also his poem "in time of daffodils(who know" and especially the lines: "in time of all sweet things beyond / whatever mind may comprehend." *E.E. Cummings: Selected Poems*, ed. Richard S. Kennedy (New York: Liveright, 1994), 181, 177.

13 From "God's Grandeur" by Gerard Manley Hopkins. We may also learn from Walt Whitman's lines from the poem "The Unexpress'd":

All human lives, throats, wishes, brains – all experiences' utterance; After the countless songs, or long or short, all tongues, all lands, Still something not yet told in poesy's voice or print – something lacking …

14 Martin Heidegger, "Hebel – Friend of the House," trans. Bruce V. Foltz and Michael Heim in *Contemporary German Philosophy*, vol. 3, ed. Darrel E. Christensen (University Park: Pennsylvania State

University Press, 1983), 89–101, esp. 94–7. Page references are to
the English translation, which is sometimes modified. Originally
published in German as "Hebel – Der Hausfreund," by Günther
Neske, Pfullingen, 1957. Later published in GA 13: 133–50. In
another proposed but undelivered talk on Hebel (May 1956),
Heidegger explicitly states in a footnote to the word *Hausfreund:*
"The house – *as house* of Being." GA 16: 546.

4. The Early Saying of Being as *Physis* (as *Aletheia*)

1 GA 75: 260.
2 See chs. 2 and 3.
3 Several thoughtful studies have been published in recent years on
   Beiträge. See, for example, the commentary of Kenneth Maly in his
   book *Heidegger's Possibility: Language, Emergence – Saying Be-ing*
   (Toronto: University of Toronto Press, 2008). Also Richard Polt,
   The Emergency of Being: On Heidegger's "Contributions to Philosophy"
   (Ithaca: Cornell University Press, 2006). Several other Heidegger
   scholars have wrestled with this text and have offered engaging
   readings; see in particular the collection of essays *Companion to
   Heidegger's "Contributions to Philosophy,"* ed. Charles E. Scott, et al.
   (Bloomington: Indiana University Press, 2001).
4 GA 40. *Introduction to Metaphysics,* trans. Gregory Fried and
   Richard Polt (New Haven: Yale University Press, 2000). Page
   references are given as (English translation: GA volume). Some
   translations are slightly modified.
5 GA 29/30. *The Fundamental Concepts of Metaphysics: World,
   Finitude, Solitude,* trans. William McNeill and Nicholas Walker
   (Bloomington: Indiana University Press, 1955). Page references are
   given as (English translation: GA volume).
6 GA 35. Translations are my own (no available English translation).
   Page references are to the GA volume only.
7 McNeill and Walker translate Heidegger's key term *Walten* as
   "prevailing," and I prefer this translation as well. In IM, Fried and Polt
   opt for "sway" in translating *Walten,* but I use "prevailing" throughout.
8 *Ajax* in *Sophocles I, Loeb Classical Library,* trans. Hugh Lloyd-
   Jones (Cambridge, MA: Harvard University Press, 1994), 90–1
   (translation modified).

9 See Fried and Polt, vii–viii.

10 In ch. 1, see especially the discussion of Heidegger's reading of Aristotle's *on hos alethes*. See also the recently published GA 73.1 (2013), esp. 132–3. He states, "Being is *the* truth as such," and observes that we have lost sight of the "truthing [*aletheuein*] of *physis* itself."

11 "On the Essence and Concept of *Physis* in Aristotle's Physics B 1," in *Pathmarks*, ed. William McNeill (Cambridge: Cambridge University Press, 1998), 230. GA 9: 301.

12 "Introduction to 'What Is Metaphysics?'" in *Pathmarks*, 283. GA 9: 373–4.

5. Sentinels of Being

1 Manuel Carbonell, born in 1918, recently died in 2011 at the age of 93. Not far from the "The Sentinel of the River" stands his thirty-six-foot-high bas-relief column "The Pillar of History," which tells the story of the Tequesta people.

2 GA 55. All page references in the chapter are to this volume; all translations are my own, unless otherwise noted. It is arguable that the trio of lecture courses on Parmenides (1942–3) and Heraclitus (1943, 1944) represent Heidegger at the height of his powers and crystallize the very essence of his thinking.

3 Manfred Frings, "Heraclitus: Heidegger's 1943 Lecture Held at Freiburg University," *Journal of the British Society for Phenomenology* 21, no. 3 (October 1990): 250–64; and "Heraclitus: Heidegger's 1944 Lecture Held at Freiburg University," *Journal of the British Society for Phenomenology* 22, no. 2 (May 1991): 65–82.

6. "This Logos Is Being Itself"

1 GA 55. All page references in the chapter are to this volume; all translations are my own, unless otherwise noted.

2 "*Logos* (*Heraklit*, Fragment 50)" in GA 7: 213–34. In translation, "*Logos* (Heraclitus, Fragment B50)" in *Early Greek Thinking*, trans. David Farrell Krell and Frank A. Capuzzi (San Francisco: Harper & Row, 1984).

3 Walt Whitman, from "Song of Myself."

4 *John of the Mountains*, 295. We may hear, too, Whitman's lines from "Song of the Open Road": "Why are there trees I never walk under but large and / melodious thoughts descend upon me? / (I think they hang there winter and summer on those trees / and always drop fruit as I pass)." And Heidegger's own words from "Out of the Experience of Thinking," GA 13: 78: "We never come to thoughts. They come to us."

Afterword

1 From "i am a little church(no great cathedral)" in *E.E. Cummings: Selected Poems*, ed. Richard S. Kennedy (New York: Liverright, 1994), 168.
2 From "The Tables Turned" by William Wordsworth.
3 GA 55: 337.
4 GA 54: 224 (Heidegger's italics).
5 In our human "sojourn," Heidegger observes, let us be able to continue to "hear the stillness" and "find our rest," and to experience the depth of the presence of all things, including "what a forest is, and a mountain meadow; what a rocky outcropping is and a cheerful, flowing stream; what a high sky is and a glittering starry night." From an address delivered by Heidegger in Todtnauberg, 30 July 1966, GA 16: 648.
6 "tiding, n.1." *The Oxford English Dictionary*, Oxford University Press.
7 A reconsideration of Heidegger's views on animals (and other living beings) is called for, and I think that a promising approach is to revisit and think through his own reflection in the 1944 lecture course on Heraclitus on the "breathing in and out" of *all beings* in relation to Being (highlighted in ch. 6).
8 *Engaging Heidegger*, chs. 5 and 6.
9 Heidegger, "On the Question Concerning the Determination of the Matter for Thinking," trans. Richard Capobianco and Marie Göbel, *Epoché* 14, no. 2 (Spring 2010): 220. GA 16: 630.

Index of Greek Terms

Index of German Terms

General Index

Anaximander, 35, 55–6, 108n7
Apollo, 74–8
Aquinas. *See* Thomas Aquinas
Arendt, Hannah, 41, 107n2
Aristotle: Aquinas, position on, 13–14, 59–60; Heidegger, influence on, 9, 12–13, 18–19, 25, 54
Artemis, 74

Beaufret, Jean, 10, 23
Being: *aletheia* (and *Aletheia*), as, 50–64, 72–4; *Anwesen*, as, 39–40; and beings (ontological difference), 30–1, 54, 107–8n3; the clearing itself, as, 16, 23–5, 49, 95, 97, 106n39; emergence, pure emerging, as, 4, 9, 11, 13, 17, 43, 49, 55, 57, 70, 73, 90, 96; *Ereignis*, as, 20–3, 38, 95–8, 106n39; *Es gibt*, as, 38–40, 95–8; exceeds Dasein and meaning, 5, 17–18, 42, 44, 63; forgottenness of, 14, 68, 77; the fundamental matter for

thought, as, 3, 11, 19, 22, 29, 38–40, 54–5; *Gegend* (*Gegnet*), as, 96; giving character of, 38–40; Greek experience of, 38–49, 109–10n7; *hen*, as, 5, 21, 25, 31, 40, 88, 94, 95; *kosmos*, as, 71–2, 101n5, 104–5n26; letting character of, 38–40, 95–8; *Lichtung*, as, 23–5, 95–8, 106n39; manifestation, as, 8, 10, 16, 37, 41–2, 71–2, 72–3, 102n7; Nature, as, 28–37, 38–49; not dependent upon Dasein, 17–18; the One, as, 25, 31, 33–5, 50–64, 67, 84–6, 88, 94; ontological condition of the possibility of meaning, as, 4–5, 11, 102n7; the Open, as, 87–9, 96; *physis* (and *Physis*), as, 18, 50–64, 71, 72–4, 77, 94; presencing, as, 19, 25, 34, 38–41, 42, 44, 48, 67–8, 108n6; the primordial *Logos*, as, 5–6, 20, 25, 39, 68, 75, 80–98; the Simple, as, 34–5, 75–6;

to-be-thought (the), 85–6
truth as (is) Being, 7–27, 60–1,
103n15, 104–5n26
truth of Being, 4, 8, 11, 16–18, 20,
25–6, 63, 74

unconcealedness, 11, 16, 93, 101,
104n18
Ur-phenomenon, 5, 19, 52, 84

Whitman, Walt, 26–7, 46, 89,
110n13, 113n4
Wittgenstein, Ludwig, 15
Wordsworth, William, 46–7, 50,
95, 110n12

New Studies in Phenomenology and Hermeneutics

General Editor: Kenneth Maly